Inventing the Truth

Inventing the Truth

THE ART AND CRAFT

OF MEMOIR

RUSSELL BAKER / ANNIE DILLARD

ALFRED KAZIN / TONI MORRISON

LEWIS THOMAS

Edited with a memoir and an introduction

by WILLIAM ZINSSER

HOUGHTON MIFFLIN COMPANY

BOSTON

1987

Library of Congress Cataloging-in-Publication Data
Inventing the truth.
1. Autobiography.   2. United States—Biography.
3. Authors, American—20th century—Biography.
I. Baker, Russell, 1925–   .   II. Zinsser,
William Knowlton.
CT25.I58   1987   973.91'092'2 [B]   87-3875
ISBN 0-395-44526-4

Printed in the United States of America
Q 10 9 8 7 6 5 4 3 2 1

Note

This book originated as a series of talks conceived and produced by Book-of-the-Month Club, Inc. The talks were held at The New York Public Library in the winter of 1986. An earlier series, held in 1985, on the art and craft of biography, resulted in the book *Extraordinary Lives*.

The Club would like to thank Vartan Gregorian, president of the Library, and David Cronin, coordinator of public education programs, for the Library's gracious collaboration as host of the series.

Two of the talks, those of Russell Baker and Toni Morrison, are followed by excerpts from the question-and-answer period that made further points about the writing process.

Contents

WILLIAM ZINSSER

Writing and

Remembering

In the early 1960s I was invited to write one-fifth of a book. The book was called *Five Boyhoods,* and it consisted of memoirs written by five men who grew up in successive decades of the twentieth century. The first chapter, by Howard Lindsay, described his turn-of-the-century boyhood in Atlantic City, a sunny Victorian world not much different from the one that he inhabited many years later as the co-author and star of one of Broadway's longest-running plays, *Life with Father.* The second chapter ("1910s"), by Harry Golden, evoked a world as cramped as Lindsay's was spacious: the dark ghetto of immigrant Jews on New York's Lower East Side. Chapter 3, on the 1920s, was by Walt Kelly, who belonged to an Irish clan that seemed to be in perpetual migration between Bridgeport and Philadelphia—hardly the twenties of F. Scott

Fitzgerald's "Jazz Age," but could Fitzgerald have created Pogo? My chapter ("1930s") was about a boyhood spent in a prosperous vale of WASPs on the north shore of Long Island, and the fifth chapter, by John Updike, recalled what it was like to grow up in the 1940s as the only child of schoolteachers in a small town in Pennsylvania; Updike's father, haunted by the fear of poverty, was glad the family lived next to a poorhouse—if necessary he could walk there.

Five boyhoods, as unalike as American boyhoods could be. Yet what struck me about the five accounts was how many themes they had in common. One was loneliness, the universal plight. Another was humor, the universal solvent. I was also struck by the fact that memory, one of the most powerful of writers' tools, is one of the most unreliable: the boy's remembered truth was often different from his parents' remembered truth. My mother, after reading my chapter, cried because my memory of my boyhood was less golden than *her* memory of my boyhood. Had I subconsciously reinvented my early years to make them lonelier than they really were? Had she subconsciously never noticed?

Mine was the most privileged of the five boyhoods. In 1920 my parents had built a large and unusually pleasant house—one of those summery, white shingled houses with a lot of screened porches—on four acres of hilly land near the end of King's Point, overlooking Manhasset Bay and Long Island Sound. Boats and water were my view; I thought it was as beautiful a location for a home as any child could ask for. My father's business in New York withstood the Depression, so my three older sisters and I were sheltered from its cold winds, and we grew up in a happy family, well loved and well provided for.

But the beautiful house was two miles from the nearest town and not near any other house. I wanted to live on a block, like everybody else, doing block things. I was also the only boy for miles around. By some Mendelian fluke, no males had been born to any of the nearby families. It was a neighborhood of girls, and that's what our house was full of: my sisters and their friends, giggling over girlish secrets, talking a language laden with mysteries. One of the first words I can remember hearing was "organdy." What did it mean? I never knew and never dared to ask.

Outflanked, I escaped into baseball. Once I entered that world of flanneled heroes I thought about little else. Sometimes during the long summers I tried to cajole the girls into playing ball. I was a proto-Charlie Brown, ever optimistic that they would catch a fly hit in their direction or throw a runner out. But no runner got thrown out. I learned very early the dismal fact that girls "throw funny." They explained that it was be-

cause their arms were "set different." Was this an ana-
tomical fact, or just another strand in the folklore of
growing up, like saltpeter in the school food and poison
at the center of the golf ball? Whatever the reason, I
was stuck with the result.

So began the solitary ballgames that were to occupy
much of my boyhood. Every day I threw a tennis ball
for hours against the side of our house, adroitly fielding
with a huge glove the line drives and grounders that
sprang out of the quivering shingles, impersonating
whole major league teams and keeping elaborate box
scores. Little did my parents, trapped inside their
booming home, realize that the person out there on the
grass wasn't me. That impeccable stylist at second base
was Charlie Gehringer of the Detroit Tigers; that ga-
zelle in the outfield was Joe DiMaggio. If my family
had only looked out the window they could have seen
greatness.

Being a baseball addict in those days was harder
work than it is today. Television hadn't been born, and
games weren't even broadcast on the radio. When I
was nine my parents sent me to a summer camp on
Cape Cod, probably hoping I would develop a fond-
ness for canoeing or some other, less tyrannical sport.
But one day at camp I made a wonderful discovery: an
announcer named Fred Hoey on a Boston radio station
did play-by-play accounts of all the home games of the

Red Sox and the Braves. How idyllic, I thought, to live near Boston; no wonder it was called the Athens of America. For years afterward I fiddled with my radio dial like a crazed ham, hoping that some atmospheric quirk would bring Hoey's magical voice through the air to me. Once I even thought I heard him, very faintly.

In such a deprived environment I subsisted on the printed word. At breakfast I gorged myself on the baseball stories and box scores in the *New York Herald Tribune* and the *New York Times*. In the evening I waited for my father to come home so that I could grab his *New York Sun*, a paper as ludicrously devoted to baseball as I was, and in between I would reread copies of *Baseball* magazine, to which I subscribed, and study with monkish dedication what was fast becoming the biggest Big League Gum collection in the East. It was from those baseball writers that I glimpsed what it might mean to be a newspaperman; they were my first "influence," the mentors who nudged me down the path to my life's work.

But the memoir that I wrote for *Five Boyhoods* was only indirectly about baseball. It was really the story of a boy contending with certain kinds of isolation. Size was another isolating factor. I was one of the smallest of boys, late to grow, living in a society of girls who shot up like mutants and were five-foot-nine by the age of twelve. Nowhere was the disparity sharper than at the dances I was made to attend throughout my youth. The tribal rules required the girls to invite the boys to these rites—another Amazonian detail—and required the boy to bring the girl a gardenia, which she would pin to the bosom of her dress. Too young to appreciate the bosom, I was just tall enough so that my nose was pressed into the gardenia I had bought to adorn it. The sickly smell of that flower was like chloroform to me as I lurched round and round the dance floor. Talk was out of the question: my partner was just as isolated and resentful. What I remember most about those nights is the quality of time standing still. I thought they literally would never end.

In *Five Boyhoods* I cloaked all these unhappy moments in humor—an old habit of mine. Humor is the writer's armor against the hard emotions—and therefore, in the case of memoir, still another distortion of the truth. Probably I also used humor as a kindness to my family. When I started writing my chapter I was half paralyzed by the awareness that my parents and my sisters were looking over my shoulder, if not actually perched there, and would read whatever version of their life came out of my typewriter. My first drafts were impossibly stiff, and though the style became warmer with each rewriting, I never really relaxed and never really enjoyed it. Since then, reading the memoirs of other writers, I've always wondered how many passengers were along on the ride, subtly altering the past.

My grandmother, my father's mother, was a stern presence in our lives. A second-generation American, she hadn't lost the Germanic relish for telling people off, and she had a copious supply of grim maxims to reinforce her point. "Kalt Kaffee macht schön," she would declare, wagging her forefinger, leaving us, as always, to deconstruct the dreadful message. "Cold coffee makes beautiful," it said, as if hot coffee were some kind of self-indulgence, or perhaps a known cause of ugliness. The maxim was a cousin of "Morgen Stund hat Gold im Mund," or "The morning hour has gold in its mouth," delivered to grandchildren who slept late. Frida Zinsser was a woman of fierce pride, bent on cultural improvement for herself and her family, and in my memoir I duly noted her strength. But I also made it clear that she was no fun.

After *Five Boyhoods* came out, my mother set me straight. " 'Grandma' wasn't really like that," she said, defending the mother-in-law who had made her own life far from easy. "She was unhappy and really quite shy, and she very much wanted to be liked." Maybe so; the truth is somewhere between my mother's version and mine. But she was like that to *me*—and that's the only truth that the writer of a memoir can work with.

All else being subjective, there was probably only one part of my memoir that I got "right"—objectively accurate to all the principal players—and that was the part about the much-loved house and the site it occupied. I described the house, with its sunlit rooms and its big windows and its agreeable porches that enabled us to watch an endless armada of boats: sailboats, motor boats, excursion boats, launches, freighters, tankers, trawlers, tugs and barges, navy destroyers and, every night at six, one of the two night steamers of the Fall River Line, aging belles named the *Priscilla* and the *Commonwealth*. I described the sounds of the water that were threaded through our lives: the chime of a bell buoy, the mournful foghorn of Execution Light, the unsteady drone of an outboard motor, which, even more than the banging of a screen door, still means summer to me. I described the hill in front of the house that we sledded down on our Flexible Flyers. One winter Long Island Sound froze over and cars drove around on the ice.

A decade after World War II my parents began to find the house hard to manage, and they sold it and moved to the city. By then quite a few of their grandchildren—my sisters' children—had played on those porches and watched those boats and heard the foghorn at night. The home had become a homestead; another generation would remember it. I only went back to see it once—in 1980, after my mother's funeral at the old family church. My own children were with me, and I drove down the once-rural road—King's Point Road—that led to our house. I could have been in any affluent suburb anywhere. The sloping fields that I remembered on both sides of the road were so dense with ranch houses and three-car garages and swimming pools that I had no sense of their topography; I only knew it in my bones.

At the end of the road, however, our house was still king of the hill. I had heard that it had changed hands several times over the years, and on this day it happened to be between occupants again. Only a contractor was there. He invited us in and took us around to show how the new owner had torn out much of the interior and was preparing to reincarnate it in Beverly Hills modern. Terrazzo squares were piled on the old wooden floors that they would soon cover; unassembled parts for several Jacuzzis awaited the plumber. Fair enough—I had no claim on the house. Its integrity was gone, but at least it was still there. I could tell my children, "This is the house I grew up in."

But the Jacuzzi man must have tired of his pleasure dome. Several years ago the house was up for sale again; my sister Nancy saw it advertised in the section of the *New York Times Magazine* that features "luxury estates." Somebody later told me it had been bought by an Iranian. I wondered how much more improving the old house could take.

Last summer an unexpected errand took me out to the family church. My wife, Caroline, was with me. I had an uneasy feeling about the house and didn't want to confront the pain of finding out what had happened to it. But Caroline urged me to put the past to rest, and once again I pointed the car down King's Point Road. At the end of the road I turned into our driveway. Something was missing: it was the house. Without the crowning house, the hill hardly seemed to be a hill; had our Flexible Flyers really hurtled down that mere incline? We walked up the former hill and stared into a huge hole where the house had been. The entire place was unkempt; it looked as if it had been abandoned for many months. I could only guess that some Iranian holding company, having cleared the land, was holding it for development.

We walked around the big hole and went and sat on the seawall. It was a perfect blue July day. The view was as beautiful as I had ever seen it. The waters of Manhasset Bay and Long Island Sound glittered in the summer sun, and there were boats as far as I could see: sailboats and power boats and fishing boats and excursion boats and freighters and tugs and barges. I heard a bell buoy and an outboard motor. I was at ease and only slightly sad. The view was intact: the unique configuration of land and sea I remember so well that I still dream about it.

But the house survived only as an act of writing.

This is a book by five Americans who have gone looking for their past with acts of writing. The book originated as a series of talks, called "The Art and Craft of Memoir," conceived by the Book-of-the-Month Club, co-sponsored by the New York Public Library and held at the library on successive Tuesday evenings in the winter of 1986. "Memoir" was defined as some portion of a life. Unlike autobiography, which moves in a dutiful line from birth to fame, omitting nothing significant, memoir assumes the life and ignores most of it. The writer of a memoir takes us back to a corner of his or her life that was unusually vivid or intense— childhood, for instance—or that was framed by unique events. By narrowing the lens, the writer achieves a focus that isn't possible in autobiography; memoir is a window into a life. What I hoped these talks would tell us was how other writers had wrestled with the form: how they had sorted out their memories and their emotions and arrived at a version of their past that they felt was true.

Russell Baker, the Pulitzer Prize-winning columnist of the *New York Times*, had written in *Growing Up* not only a superb memoir; it was a classic book about the

Depression—a perfect illustration of the fact that a good memoir is also a work of history, catching a distinctive moment in the life of both a person and a society. Baker's memoir took strength from its public context.

Annie Dillard, the author of *Pilgrim at Tinker Creek* and five other books, is writing a memoir called *An American Childhood*, in which she places her lively Pittsburgh childhood in the larger frame of the American landscape, "the vast setting of our common history." Her memoir, she says, is "about waking up"— about what it feels like to "notice that you've been set down in a going world."

Alfred Kazin, dean of American literary critics, has written three memoirs covering successive phases of his life, the most enduring being *A Walker in the City*, which dealt with his childhood as the son of immigrant Jews in the Brownsville section of Brooklyn. I still remember how sensual that book was. Kazin wrote with his nose, making me smell what his mother was cooking for the Sabbath dinner—when, at sundown, "a healing quietness would come over Brownsville"—and how his father's overalls smelled of shellac and turpentine when he came home from his job as a housepainter. Seldom has a writer put memory to such evocative use.

Toni Morrison is a novelist and therefore not usually identified with memoir, a nonfiction form. Yet memory is one of the animating currents of her work, and few American writers have tapped it with such richness of language. In her novels such as *Song of Solomon* we hear voices far older than her own: the fragments of recollection and imagery and handed-down lore that constitute the black oral tradition. "When I think of things my mother or father or aunts used to say," she once remarked, "it seems the most absolutely striking thing in the world."

Lewis Thomas, with *Lives of a Cell*, caught the attention of American readers in 1974 as a born writer and as that even rarer species—the scientist who is a humanist. In a subsequent book, *The Youngest Science*, the life cycle that Dr. Thomas studied was his own, and the result was a double memoir: the coming of age of an American doctor and the coming of age of American medicine. In its early chapters he recalled accompanying his father, a general practitioner, on his rounds in the days when medicine was "a profoundly ignorant occupation" and his father carried only four medications in his black bag because they were the only ones that were known to do any good. Reading it, I thought, "I'm glad *I* wasn't treated by those doctors." Then I remembered, "I *was* treated by those doctors." Memoir puts lives in perspective, not only for the writer but for the rest of us.

The sixth writer in the series, William L. Shirer, had

to drop out because of illness. Shirer, whose *The Rise and Fall of the Third Reich* is the Book-of-the-Month Club's all-time best-seller, recently returned to that theme in *The Nightmare Years, 1930–1940*, this time telling the story in the form of a memoir, recalling how that nightmarish decade looked to a young foreign correspondent. All his life Shirer had been a reporter and a writer of history; now, in his old age, he was putting the same events in the frame of personal experience. "I think most of us in this business want to have a final say," he told me, "because we never had time to stop and ask what it all meant. And I'm sure there are other reasons, like egotism, which you deny having." Deny it or not, it's there. Ego is at the heart of all the reasons why anybody writes a memoir, whether it's a book or a pamphlet or a letter to our children. Memoir is how we validate our lives.

These were some of the suppositions that went into the talks. What came out of them were five trips to the well of memory that touched deep emotions. One central point also emerged: the writer of a memoir must become the editor of his own life. He must cut and prune an unwieldy story and give it a narrative shape. His duty is to the reader, not to himself. "The autobiographer's problem," Russell Baker says, "is that he knows much too much; he knows the whole iceberg, not just the tip." Annie Dillard says, "The writer of any first-person work must decide two obvious questions: what to put in and what to leave out."

Nor is it enough just to decide what to put in; fidelity to the facts is no free pass to the reader's attention, as Russell Baker discovered when he approached the writing of *Growing Up* with the reflexes of a lifelong journalist. What he wrote was "a reporter's book," one in which he faithfully re-created the Depression era after interviewing all his older relatives who had lived through it. What he left out, with a good reporter's propriety, was his mother and himself—in short, the story. Reviewing that disastrous first version, he saw that the only chapter that had vitality was one about an uncle who had largely invented the story of his life to make it more colorful. The lesson was not lost on the nephew. When Baker rewrote his memoir it became a dramatic story about an "extremely strong woman and weak male." How much of that drama was artifice? I only know that it felt true.

Toni Morrison, another searcher for truth in the buried past, also knows that it can only be quarried by an act of imagination. She takes as her literary heritage the slave narratives written in the eighteenth and nineteenth centuries to persuade white Americans that blacks were "worthy of God's grace and the immediate abandonment of slavery." But because those writers wanted to elevate the argument and not anger their masters, they "dropped a veil" over the terrible details of their daily existence; no trace of their thoughts and emotions can be found. Toni Morrison wants access to that interior life—it contains the truth about her past that she needs for her work. She can only get it by imagining it: by an act of writing. Unlike Russell Baker, heightening reality to give it the drama of fiction, Toni Morrison uses fiction to conjure up what was real. Both of them have skipped over research and landed on the truth.

Putting all this in formal terms, Annie Dillard says, "My advice to memoir writers is to embark on a memoir for the same reason that you would embark on any other book: to fashion a text." The advice sounds too academic; we like to think that a good life will fashion itself into a text. It won't. We like to think that Thoreau went back to Concord after his sojourn at Walden Pond and just wrote up his notes. He didn't. He wrote seven different drafts of *Walden* in eight years, finally piecing together by what Margaret Fuller called the "mosaic" method a book that strikes us as casual and even chatty. Probably no classic of American literature was more deliberately fashioned. Thoreau was not a woodsman by vocation when he went to the woods for a year; he was a writer, and he wrote one of our sacred texts. By the time he had written it, in fact, he had almost surely forgotten what he did at Walden Pond. If you prize your memories, Annie Dillard says, don't write a memoir—the act of writing about an experience takes so much longer and is so much more intense than the experience itself that you're left only with what you have written, just as the snapshots of your vacation become more real than your vacation. You have cannibalized your remembered truth and replaced it with a new one.

For Alfred Kazin, the son of Russian Jews, these finicky exercises in memoir—Thoreau's *Walden*, Emerson's journals and essays, *The Education of Henry Adams*, Whitman's *Leaves of Grass* and his Civil War diary, *Specimen Days*—were the door that he walked through to claim his own American heritage. What struck him was how personal these writers were; they used the most intimate literary forms to place themselves in the landscape of American history. Their books brought Kazin the news that was to shape his life: "One could be a writer without writing a novel. Every taxi driver and bartender who told you his story wanted to be a novelist. It was the expected, the Big Thing, in America." It was not the Big Thing to Kazin. He recalls that Leslie Fiedler, in his review of *A Walker in the City*, found it perverse that the book "obstinately refuses to become a novel."

Personal history is the one true form for Kazin. He

tells us that since he was a boy he has started every day by pouring into his journal "everything that I felt like describing and writing about." It was, he says, "some effort to think my life out." But it was also an effort to think his way into the heart and mind of the country that he was born in. His daily journal became "a cherished connection with something fundamental to American literature—the writing of personal history: diaries, journals, letters, memoirs. The influence of Puritanism had created a habit of mind that had persisted into the 'American Renaissance' and the peculiarly personal reverberations in Emerson, Thoreau, Whitman and how many others—the need to present to God, the Eternal Reader and Judge of the soul's pilgrimage on earth, the veritable record of one's inner life." Obviously Kazin took this habit with him when he wrote *A Walker in the City* and its sequels, *Starting Out in the Thirties* and *New York Jew*. Memoir was his way of planting his roots alongside those of his literary idols in the memoir-rich American soil.

No such connections matter to Lewis Thomas. In his chronometry, centuries rise and fall in a flicker and nationality has no meaning. Dr. Thomas is by training a cell biologist, and when he turns reminiscent he thinks of himself as a collection of cells. What massive division of cells went into his being here at all? What miracle of cellular activity enabled this bundle of cells to acquire the gift of language? "It is because of language," he says, "that I am able now to think farther back into my lineage, to the family stories of Welshmen, back into the shadows when all the Welsh were kings," back to the beginnings of writing (maybe 10,000 years), back to the beginnings of speech ("100,000 years, give or take 50,000"), back to . . . where? Ask a cell biologist to talk about memoir and he won't be satisfied until he gets back to the original bacterial cell. "We are all," he concludes, "in the same family: grasses, seagulls, fish, fleas and voting citizens of the republic."

What a trip Lewis Thomas takes us on! It is a journey of unimaginable length—nothing less than a memoir of life on earth. At the end, however, his thoughts turn back to the collection of cells known as *Homo sapiens.* "I am," he says, "a member of a fragile species, here only a few moments as evolutionary time is measured, a juvenile species. We are only tentatively set in place, error-prone, at risk of fumbling, in real danger at the moment of leaving behind only a thin layer of our fossils, radioactive at that."

Like every good practitioner of memoir, he has placed himself in context.

RUSSELL BAKER

Life with Mother

I'm primarily a journalist, a commercial writer, and I find it odd to be talking as a memoirist. Memoirs are for remembrance. And the remembrances of journalists, when they take book form, are what I think of as "and then I met" books. In my time as a journalist I have met many what we call great men—at least celebrated men. But in *Growing Up* I was not interested in doing an "and then I met" book. My prime interest was to celebrate people whom nobody had ever heard of. And whom I was terribly fond of, for the most part, and thought deserved to be known.

Why did I write this book? I asked my daughter the other day, "What should I say when I talk at the Public Library next week?" And she said, "You should say why you thought you had something so interesting to say that a large number of people would want to read it." And I said I hadn't anticipated that any number of people would want to read it; what I'd wanted was to write a book that I felt I had to write. It grew out of a number of things that had been happening in my life, perhaps starting at birth. As a writer I was blessed from the cradle, because I had the good fortune to be born into two very large, some people would say immense, families. The sort they don't make anymore.

My father was one of thirteen children, twelve of whom were boys. My mother was one of nine children, seven of whom were boys. So I came into the world well equipped with uncles. Twenty of them—that is, if you count my uncle Emil and my uncle Harold, who married Aunt Sally and Aunt Sister, respectively. What's more, a lot of these uncles got married, and this has provided me with a healthy supply of aunts. Now if you're destined to have a not very interesting life— and I was so destined—the next best thing, if you're going to be a writer, is to have a huge family. It gives you a chance to learn a lot about humanity from close-up observation.

I worry about people who get born nowadays, because they get born into such tiny families—sometimes into no family at all. When you're the only pea in the pod, your parents are likely to get you confused with the Hope Diamond. And that encourages you to talk too much. Getting into the habit of talking too much is fine if you're destined to be a lawyer or a politician or an entertainer. But if you're going to be a writer, it's death. We have many writers nowadays who don't realize this. Writers have to cultivate the habit early in life of listening to people other than themselves. And if you're born into a big family, as I was, you might as well learn to listen, because they're not going to give you much chance to talk. With twenty uncles and a dozen aunts, all old enough to have earned the right to speak whenever they wanted to open their mouths, there was not a great demand for us three children to put in our oar and to liven up the discussion.

I've never been able to complete an accurate count of the number of cousins I have. But I have cousins to the utmost degree. In addition to first cousins, I have second, third and fourth cousins, plus cousins many times removed. I have first cousins who are old enough to be my parents, and I have first cousins young enough to be my children. I'm constantly discovering cousins who were born when my attention was diverted somewhere else. Just recently I learned that the star of the Johns Hopkins lacrosse team is the great-grandson of my first cousin Myrtle, which I suppose makes him my great-grandcousin.

Now I cite these battalions of relatives not to boast about the fertility of my blood line, but to illustrate why I spent most of my childhood learning to listen.

When the grown-ups in a family that big said that children were born to be seen and not heard, they weren't just exercising the grown-up right to engage in picturesque speech and tired old maxims. Nor were they trying to stifle children's right to creative expression. For them holding down the uproar was a question of survival. And it was wonderful training if you are going to be a writer: having to give up the right to show off and be a childhood performer and just sit there, quietly watching and listening to the curious things grown-ups did and said.

Out of this experience, at least in my family, there grew a kind of home folklore tradition, which was sustained among those of us who had been children together—a habit of reminiscent storytelling, whenever we got together, about what we remembered from childhood. About the lives, deeds, sayings and wisdom of elders. About aunts, uncles, grandparents, great-aunts, strangers who would come courting, women who—as the phrase always went—put up with an awful lot.

Putting up with an awful lot was what women seemed to do in the days of my childhood. My cousin Lillian, who was nearly eighty when I interviewed her for *Growing Up* about my mother's relationship with my father, said, "Well, Russell, people said Betty was hard to get along with. But she had to put up with an awful lot." Indeed she did. I had my own stock of these family tales and was fond, when dining out and the wine was flowing a little too generously, of telling the company about the time my grandmother Baker scolded a visiting delegation of the Ku Klux Klan for making a mess of their mothers' bed sheets. Or the time the Jersey City cops arrested Uncle Jim for running a red light and took away his shoelaces so he wouldn't try to hang himself in the cell. With that many uncles you had a great variety of material.

My editor, Tom Congdon, was present at a few of these dinners when I was telling old stories, and after a while he began cajoling me to put them into some kind of book about what it was like growing up in an antique time in a big family. He began referring to it as "the growing up book." Of course I had no intention of writing it. I was already turning out a newspaper column three times a week, which meant grinding out a hundred thousand words a year for my job. Spending my leisure writing another couple of hundred thousand words was hardly my idea of amusement.

But long before Tom started stirring the creative waters, something had begun to bother me. To wit, middle age. My children arrived at adolescence in the 1960s—that slum of a decade—and the 1970s, not one of the vintage decades either. And I was dismayed to observe, as elderly folk usually do when the children hit adolescence, that the values I'd been bred to cherish and live by were now held in contempt by people of my children's age. What was even worse, those values were regarded as squalid—remnants of the despicable, social-political system that my generation had connived in creating for the suppression of freedom.

It seemed to me that these views came out of a profound ignorance of history. Not uncommon among adolescents. As I vaguely recalled from my own experience, adolescence was a time when you firmly believed that sex hadn't been invented until the year you started high school, when the very idea that anything interesting might have happened during your parents' lifetime was unthinkable. I knew because I had been an adolescent myself. I remembered how ludicrous I thought it was that anybody could have tolerated spending their youth in the dreary decades of Theodore Roosevelt, Woodrow Wilson and World War I, as my parents had.

With my children in this insufferable phase of life it became harder and harder to speak with them as a father ought to speak to his children. When I corrected them and undertook to advise them on how to do things right, I took my example from the way things were done in my days. Which produced a great deal of invisible but nevertheless palpable sneering. Adolescence was finishing its nasty work of turning them from dear sweet children into the same ornery people you meet every day as you go through life. The kind of people who insist on disagreeing with you. And behaving like people.

In the hope of breaking through that communications blackout I tried writing a few letters to them. Just a few. For I soon realized that these were the kind of letters that bore the eyes right out of an adolescent. They were long descriptions of my own childhood, in which I tried to convey to them some sense of how different and remote was the world that I had come from; to tell them about their own forebears, who had lived and died before they were born, so they might glean at least a hint that life was more than a single journey from the diaper to the shroud. I wanted my children to know that they were part of a long chain of humanity extending deep into the past and that they had some responsibility for extending it into the future.

Going through the carbons of some old correspondence recently, I was astonished to come across a couple of these letters that I had written the kids a long time ago and to recognize long blocks of writing that would appear again, not much changed, in *Growing Up*, which I wrote ten years later. And I realized that I'd been writing that book to my children long before Tom Congdon heard me writing it over the wine at dinner.

But what finally prompted the book to become a book was what I came to think of as the living death of my mother—whose mind went out one day as though every circuit in the city had been blown. I was in Key West at the time; my sister Doris called me and told me what had happened, and I flew up to Baltimore and went to the hospital—completely unprepared for what I was going to encounter. And I started talking to my mother, and she was completely gone. I was speechless. She was suffering from something that I have since come to recognize as very common to elderly folks but that I had never seen before and certainly had never thought would happen to my mother. I was so astonished that my only reaction was to start taking notes on what she was saying. I had stopped at the hospital gift shop, as people sometimes do, to take some knickknack up to her, not realizing what I was going to find, and I tore the paper bag open so that I could write on the back of it. And I started making a record of our conversation. It's a reporter's reflex. What I was hearing was so amazing that I instinctively began recording it on the back of this bag. When I left I stuffed it in a raincoat pocket and forgot about it. I found it many weeks later and put it in a desk drawer and again I forgot it for a long time. And that turned out to be the conversation that appears in the first chapter of *Growing Up*—that disjointed conversation.

When I realized what had happened to my mother I was in a kind of intellectual shock, and I didn't know how to deal with it for a long time. Gradually it seemed to me that the way to deal with it was to write about the times that the two of us had passed through together. And I began to do that. But being the good reporter, I had no concept of how to write a memoir. I knew nothing about it; I only knew how to report a magazine piece. So I took my tape recorder out and I interviewed many of my relatives, those who were still living—people in their eighties, one or two in their nineties—about the family, things I had never been interested in before. And my wife Mimi and I began doing the genealogy. Who were these people? I had no notion of who they were or where they had come from. And in the process I began to learn how interesting they were. They were people who would be extremely boring to read about in the newspaper, but they were fascinating. And I transcribed all these interviews and notes. I reported everything very carefully: a long piece of newspaper reportage. Then I started writing, and what I wrote was a reporter's book in which I quoted these elderly people talking about what life was like long ago in that time and place. I was reporting my own life and, being the good journalist, I kept myself out of it. And because I was uneasy about what had always been an awkward relationship with my mother and because she wasn't there to testify for herself, I kept *her* out of it. And I wrote a rather long book. I think it ran to four hundred and fifty pages in manuscript.

I was very pleased with it and I sent it off to my agent and my editor and I thought, "Well, I'll give them twenty-four hours to sit up all night and read it and they'll phone me back tomorrow." You always have that feeling of euphoria just about having finished any-thing. Well, there was no phone call the next day, nor the day after. Nobody called the next week, nor the week after that. A month passed and nobody called. By then Tom Congdon had his own publishing company, and I knew he was in financial trouble, and I told myself, "Tom is too busy trying to raise money to bother reading this great manuscript." And I put it in the drawer and forgot it.

Eventually I began to sense that there was something wrong, and one night I took it out of the drawer and sat down in my office and started to read. I nodded off on about page 20. And I thought, "If I can't read this thing . . ." But it was an intensely responsible book. Everything in it was correct, the quotations were accu-rate, everything had been double-checked. Finally, Tom, in despair, asked for a conference. Tom and I had worked together a long time, but he has never quite figured out how to tell me something is no good, and to tell somebody that a whole book is no good is tough for any editor, I guess.

But by that time I had made a second judgment myself that the book was in terrible shape and I knew what was wrong with it: my mother wasn't in it. There were all these interesting relatives, the uncles and the aunts and people talking from the present about the old days, but it was really nothing but journalism—reminiscences of today about yesterday. I had lunch with Tom and I said that I knew what was wrong with the book and that I would rewrite the whole thing. I said it was a book about a boy and his mother. It was about the tension between a child and his mother, and everything had to hinge on that. And Tom said he thought that was right—that I had made a grievous mistake in trying to write a book about myself in which I didn't appear. He didn't realize the strength of the mother character as I did, and I knew that if I brought the mother in and made her the hinge on which everything swung, the book would be a story. It would work as a book. I told Tom that's what I intended to do.

Now at one point Tom gave me a piece of advice, and I pass it on to any of you who are tempted someday to write your memoir. As I say, I had given Tom this manuscript of faithfully reported history of what people remembered of the '20s and '30s, and in it I had written what I thought was a good chapter about my uncle Harold. It's the one that begins: "Uncle Harold was famous for lying." And I knew that was a good chapter because I "got" Uncle Harold—I turned him into a character. I hadn't reported him; I made him the man whose memory lived inside me. At some point in the book I made a conclusion about him: I said that Uncle Harold, an uneducated and an unread man, was famous for being a great liar. But he wasn't really a liar; he just wanted life to be more interesting than it was. He lived a very dull life—he was a gravedigger at that time—and he liked to tell stories, but he didn't tell them very well. I said that in his primitive way Uncle Harold had perceived that the possibilities of achieving art lie not in reporting, but in fiction. And Tom Congdon sent that page back to me underlined in red, and he wrote on it, "I honor Uncle Harold."

Well, the problem that I knew, and that Tom didn't know at the time I resolved to rewrite the book, was that I had been dishonest about my mother. What I had written, though it was accurate to the extent that the reporting was there, was dishonest because of what I had left out. I had been unwilling to write honestly. And that dishonesty left a great hollow in the center of the original book.

Funny things happen to you when you really start to research something like this. I made a couple of serendipitous discoveries. One was that . . . well, my mother kept a trunk. I knew that. All good Southern ladies kept a trunk that they carried with them through life, and my mother was no exception. When she became incompetent, my sister took custody of this trunk, but my sister has no interest in that sort of thing, and she called my younger son, who was a pack rat, and told him to come over and take anything he was interested in out of it.

He was delighted. He went through the trunk and he came back with, among other things, a series of love letters that had been sent to my mother in the years 1932 and 1933, the depths of the Depression, by an immigrant Dane named Oluf. I had never known that she was in love with this man. It was obviously an unconsummated love affair because he was away most of the time. He moved to western Pennsylvania and they never saw each other after the most casual encounters.

Now I knew that what I was writing was a book about the Depression, and yet I dreaded having to write about it. Writing about the Depression is extremely dull—everybody knows the statistics, and I couldn't figure out any way to make this interesting. And yet the Depression was the very essence of the setting of this book. I kept worrying about how I was going to handle the Depression chapter. I made several passes at it, writing in terms of statistical reports. Then my son went through my mother's trunk and found Oluf's letters. They were almost illegible—he wrote in a fractured English that was hard to read, in a big flowing script, and there were many of these letters. I gave them to my wife. I said, "Read these and tell me if there's anything in them," and I went off to work. That evening when I got home she was visibly moved. She said, "This is the story of a man who was destroyed by the Depression."

So I read them, and it was the most moving story. It was a self-contained story. And while I was moved, I was also delighted, because it had solved my Depression problem. Here was what the Depression meant to one man. That made a chapter which cleared up a lot of problems and some mysteries about my mother.

The second serendipitous discovery that came from that trunk was my mother's marriage certificate, which my son brought me in Nantucket. He paid me a surprise call. One summer day I was sitting in the backyard sunning myself, and my son came in the yard grinning. "You won't guess what I've got," he said. It was my mother's marriage certificate. And I looked at it: she was married in March of the year in which I was born in August. I was fifty-four years old and I realized I was a love child.

Well, it made me feel a little more interesting than I was. And it also cleared up a number of things— mysteries that I hadn't been able to solve in the first version of the book. Why my mother and my grandmother (my father's mother) detested each other so deeply. Why my mother left that part of the world so rapidly after my father died. The morning she learned that he was dead, she called her brother in New Jersey and announced that she was going to come live with him.

All of these things that had left me utterly baffled suddenly fell into place. And then I realized, too, why she had opposed so deeply my own relationship with the woman who was ultimately to be my wife. Everything fell into place, made a story. The question was, Could I write this? I hadn't written it in the book, and it made that first book a lie. So, in revising, I determined I would write that story. I thought, "If I want to honor my mother in this book I must be truthful." But I did it with great trepidation. Because you could be accused of vulgarity, of airing dirty linen and exploiting your dying mother for commercial purposes. And yet I felt that it dishonored her to lie about it.

So I decided to do it. I decided that although nobody's life makes any sense, if you're going to make a book out of it you might as well make it into a story. I remember saying to my wife, "I am now going upstairs to invent the story of my life." And I started writing, on the days when I wasn't doing my column, and I rewrote that whole book—almost the entire thing, with the exception of a couple of chapters—in about six months. That was the book that was eventually published.

But first I took the manuscript to my sister Doris—the two of us had grown up together—and had her read it. I anticipated that she was going to raise violent objections to my mentioning the fact that my mother had been pregnant before her marriage. And she did object, but not violently. Rationally, she said she thought that was a disgraceful thing to publish about Mother. And I told her pretty much what I've just told you: that I thought honesty would serve my mother best in the long run; it would make her plausible in this book, in which she might live longer than most of us if it worked right. And that anyhow, nowadays, nobody cared. "So be it," said Doris, and we published.

Still, I was very worried about the public reaction. God knows what was going to happen about that. I worried about that more than about anything else in the book. And I remember being deeply moved the day the *Wall Street Journal* ran its review, which was by Michael Gartner. The first sentence began: "Russell Baker's mother, a miraculous woman . . ."

———

Q. What were the reactions of your children?

A. I don't know. Although we are very close to our children, there are certain things children don't tell their parents. The children liked the book, surely. And they were proud of it, I think. My daughter, our oldest, said she was grateful for the book because it gave her her grandmother, whom she had only known when she was a baby.

Q. How much of your book is truthful and how much is good writing?

A. Well, all the incidents are truthful. A book like that has certain things in common with fiction. Anything that is autobiographical is the opposite of biography. The biographer's problem is that he never knows enough. The autobiographer's problem is that he knows much too much. He knows absolutely everything; he knows the whole iceberg, not just the tip. I mean, Henry James knew all the things that have puzzled Leon Edel for years; he knew what that tragic moment was that happened. So when you're writing about yourself, the problem is what to leave out. And I just left out almost everything—there's only about half a percent in that book. You wouldn't want everything; it would be like reading the *Congressional Record*. But the incidents that *are* in the book, of course they happened.

For example, there's a long account of the day of my father's death, which occurred when I was five. People said, "How could you have known that?" I knew that. That was the first thing I knew. That whole day began to happen as if I was sitting in the theater of life and the curtain was going up. It was the start of my life. I can still hear people talking that day. I know what the air smelled like. I know what people's faces looked like. How they were dressed. What they were eating. Don't ask me what I did yesterday—I'd have to look in my diary—but *that* I knew. I didn't do anything in the book that wasn't right.

Q. How did you decide what to put in and what to leave out?

A. I decided that the story line was the mother and the son: this extremely strong woman and weak male. There are three strong women in the book—the grandmother, the mother and the woman that the son marries at the end—and it's the story of the tension that these various women put on each other and on the male figure. I don't have a lot in the book that doesn't contribute to that point of view of what the story material was.

Q. I wanted to ask you about another woman in the book that I found unforgettable: your wife. Was she in the first version as she was in the book that I read?

A. She didn't appear in the first version. Because of the business about my mother and my birth, I didn't need Mimi. I didn't want to go that far. But I finally saw that to make the book an integral work I needed her—she was the logical completion of the series of events that started with my birth. I hated to use the material because it was material for another book that

I'd often thought of writing. And I threw it away in ten or fifteen thousand words.

Mimi was a good sport, though. When I told her that I thought the book needed this, she was very supportive. I said, "Do you mind if I write about it?" and she said, "No, go ahead." And I interviewed her just the way I did everybody else. She was a terrible interview. She lied like a politician. But I interviewed her and I went up and wrote those concluding chapters. They went very quickly. And I brought it to her finally and said, "Read through it, and if there's anything you want cut, I'll cut it." Well, after reading it she said she thought I had left out certain events that would make it more interesting. I was sort of shocked at some of the things she suggested ought to be added, and I said, "Look, I'm a writer who's used to dealing with sensitive material—let me make the decision." And my decision was not to add a thing.

Well, after several months we got the first copies of the book in the mail, and Mimi immediately grabbed one, took it to the bedroom, closed the door and read all afternoon. When she came out she looked appalled. "Well, what do you think?" I said to her, and she said, "It looks different in print."

"That's what they always say," I told her.

ANNIE DILLARD

To Fashion a Text

I'm here because I'm writing a book called *An American Childhood*, which is a memoir—insofar as a memoir is any account, usually in the first person, of incidents that happened a while ago. It isn't an autobiography, and it isn't "memoirs." I wouldn't dream of writing my memoirs; I'm only forty years old. Or my autobiography; any chronology of my days would make very dull reading—I've spent about thirty years behind either a book or a desk. The book that I'm writing is an account of a childhood in Pittsburgh, Pennsylvania, where I grew up.

The best memoirs, I think, forge their own forms. The writer of any work, and particularly any nonfiction work, must decide two crucial points: what to put in and what to leave out.

So I thought, "What shall I put in?" Well, what is

the book about? *An American Childhood* is about the passion of childhood. It's about a child's vigor, and originality, and eagerness, and mastery, and joy.

It's about waking up. A child wakes up over and over again, and notices that she's living. She dreams along, loving the exuberant life of the senses, in love with beauty and power, oblivious of herself—and then suddenly, bingo, she wakes up and feels herself alive. She notices her own awareness. And she notices that she is set down here, mysteriously, in a going world. The world is full of fascinating information that she can collect and enjoy. And the world is public; its issues are moral and historical ones.

So the book is about two things: a child's interior life —vivid, superstitious and timeless—and a child's growing awareness of the world. The structural motion of the book is from the interior landscape—one brain's own idiosyncratic topography—to the American landscape, the vast setting of our common history. The little child pinches the skin on the back of her hand and sees where God made Adam from spit and clay. The older child explores the city on foot and starts to work on her future as a detective, or an epidemiologist, or a painter. Older yet, she runs wild and restless over the city's bridges, and finds in Old Testament poetry and French symbolist poetry some language sounds she loves.

The interior life is in constant vertical motion; consciousness runs up and down the scales every hour like a slide trombone. It dreams down below; it notices up above; and it notices itself, too, and its own alertness. The vertical motion of consciousness, from inside to outside and back, interests me. I've written about it once before, in an essay about a solar eclipse, and I wanted to do more with it.

For a private interior life, I've picked—almost at random—my own. As an aside, this isn't as evident as it may seem. I simply like to write books. About twelve years ago, while I was walking in Acadia National Park in Maine, I decided to write a narrative—a prose narrative, because I wanted to write prose. After a week's thought I decided to write mostly about nature, because I thought I could make it do what I wanted, and I decided to set it all on the coast of Maine. I decided further to write it in the third person, about a man, a sort of metaphysician, in his fifties. A month or so later I decided reluctantly to set the whole shebang in Virginia, because I knew more about Virginia. Then I decided to write it in the first person, as a man. Not until I had written the first chapter and showed it around—this was *Pilgrim at Tinker Creek*—did I give up the pretext of writing in the first person as a man. I wasn't out to deceive people; I just didn't like the idea of writing about myself. I knew I wasn't the subject.

So in this book, for simplicity's sake, I've got my own interior life. It was a lively one. I put in what it was that had me so excited all the time—the sensation of time pelting me as if I were standing under a waterfall. I loved the power of the life in which I found myself. I loved to feel its many things in all their force. I put in what it feels like to play with the skin on your mother's knuckles. I put in what it feels like to throw a baseball—you aim your whole body at the target and watch the ball fly off as if it were your own head. I put in drawing pencil studies of my baseball mitt and collecting insects and fooling around with a microscope.

In my study on Cape Cod, where I write, I've stuck above my desk a big photograph of a little Amazonian boy whose face is sticking out of a waterfall or a rapids. White water is pounding all around his head, in a kind of wreath, but his face is absolutely still, looking up, and his black eyes are open dreamily on the distance. That little boy is completely alive; he's letting the mystery of existence beat on him. He's having his childhood, and I think he knows it. And I think he will come out of the water strong, and ready to do some good. I see this photograph whenever I look up from my computer screen.

So I put in that moment of waking up and noticing that you've been put down in a world that's already under way. The rushing of time wakes you: you play along mindless and eternal on the kitchen floor, and time streams in full flood beside you on the floor. It rages beside you, down its swollen banks, and when it wakes you you're so startled you fall in.

When you wake up, you notice that you're here.

"Here," in my case, was Pittsburgh. I put in the three rivers that meet here. The Allegheny from the north and the Monongahela from the south converge to form the Ohio, the major tributary of the Mississippi, which, in turn, drains the whole continent east of the divide via the Missouri River rising in the Rocky Mountains. The great chain of the Alleghenies kept pioneers out of Pittsburgh until the 1760s, one hundred and fifty years after Jamestown.

I put in those forested mountains and hills, and the way the three rivers lie flat and moving among them, and the way the low land lies wooded among them, and the way the blunt mountains rise in the darkness from the rivers' banks.

I put in Lake Erie, and summers along its mild shore. I put in New Orleans, the home of Dixieland jazz, where my father was heading when he jumped in his boat one day to go down the river like Huck Finn.

I put in the pioneers who "broke wilderness," and the romance of the French and Indian Wars that centered around Fort Duquesne and Fort Pitt. I put in the brawling rivermen—the flatboatmen and keelboatmen.

I put in the old Scotch-Irish families who dominate Pittsburgh and always have. The Mellons are Scotch-Irish, and so were Andrew Carnegie and Henry Clay Frick. They're all Presbyterians. I grew up in this world—at the lunatic fringe of it—and it fascinates me. I think it's important. I think it's peculiarly American —that mixture of piety and acquisitiveness, that love of work. They're Calvinists, of course—just like the Massachusetts Puritans—and I think I can make a case that their influence on American thought was greater than the Puritans'. There were far more Scotch-Irish Presbyterians, after all, and they settled all over the American colonies and carried their democracy and pragmatism with them.

In Pittsburgh the Scotch-Irish constitute a world of many families whose forebears knew each other, who respect each other's discretion and who admire each other for occupying their slots without fuss. The men are withdrawn, the women are ironic. They believe in their world; they all stay in Pittsburgh, and their children stay there. I alone am escaped to tell thee. I and David McCullough, who grew up a few houses away. And James Laughlin, the publisher. All of us Pittsburgh Scotch-Irish Presbyterians.

My sisters and I grew up in this world, and I put it in *An American Childhood*. I put in our private school and quiet club and hushed neighborhood where the houses were stone and their roofs were slate. I put in dancing with little boys at dancing school, and looking at the backs of their interesting necks at Presbyterian church.

Just to make trouble, I put in money. My grandmother used to tell me never to touch money with my bare hands.

I put in books, for that's where this book started, with an essay I wrote for the *New York Times Magazine* on reading books. Almost all of my many passionate interests, and my many changes of mind, came through books. Books prompted the many vows I made to myself. Nonfiction books lured me away from the world —as I dreamed about working for Scotland Yard, doing field work in freshwater streams, rock collecting in the salt desert, painting in Paris. And novels dragged me back into the world—because I would read whatever was handy, and what was handy in those years were novels about the Second World War. I read so many books about the Second World War that I knew how to man a minesweeper before I knew how to walk in high heels. You couldn't read much about the war without figuring out that the world was a moral arena that required your strength.

I had the notion back then that everything was interesting if you just learned enough about it. Now, writing about it, I have the pleasure of learning it all again and finding that it *is* interesting. I get to inform myself and any readers about such esoterica as rock collecting, which I hadn't thought about in almost thirty years.

When I was twelve a paperboy gave me two grocery bags full of rock and mineral chunks. It took me most of a year to identify them. At a museum shop I bought cards of what they called thumbnail specimens. And I read books about a fairly absurd batch of people who called themselves rockhounds; they spent their evenings in the basement sawing up slabs of travertine into wavy slices suitable, they said, for wall hangings.

Now, in this memoir, I get to recall where the romance of rock collecting had lain: the symbolic sense that underneath the dreary highways, underneath Pittsburgh, were canyons of crystals—that you could find treasure by prying open the landscape. In my reading I learned that people have cracked knobs of granite and laid bare clusters of red garnets and topaz crystals, chrysoberyl, spudomene and emerald. They held in their hands crystals that had hung in a hole in the dark for a billion years unseen. I liked the idea of that. I would lay about me right and left with a hammer and bash the landscape to bits. I would crack the earth's crust like a piñata and spread its vivid prizes in chunks to the light. That's what I wanted to do. So I put that in.

It's also a great pleasure to write about my parents, because they're both great storytellers—comedians, actually—which gives me a chance to tell their wonderful stories. We were all young, at our house, and we enjoyed ourselves.

My father was a dreamer; he lived differently from other men around him. One day he abruptly quit the family firm—when I was ten—and took off down the Ohio River in a boat by himself to search out the roots of jazz in New Orleans. He came back after several months and withdrew from corporate life forever. He knew the world well—all sort of things, which he taught us to take an interest in: how people build bridge pilings in the middle of a river, how jazz came up the river to be educated in Chicago, how the pioneers made their way westward from Pittsburgh, down the Ohio River, sitting on the tops of their barges and singing "Bang Away, My Lulu."

My mother was both a thinker and what one might call a card. If she lay on the beach with friends and found the conversation dull, she would give a little push with her heel and roll away. People were stunned. She rolled deadpan and apparently effortlessly, her arms and legs extended tidily, down the beach to the distant water's edge where she lay at ease just as she had been, but half in the surf, and well out of earshot. She was not only a card but a wild card, a force for disorder.

She regarded even tiny babies as straight men, and liked to step on the drawstring of a crawling baby's gown, so that the baby crawled and crawled and never got anywhere except into a little ball at the top of the gown.

She was interested in language. Once my father and I were in the kitchen listening to a ballgame—the Pirates playing the New York Giants. The Giants had a utility infielder named Wayne Terwilliger. Just as Mother walked through the kitchen, the announcer said, "Terwilliger bunts one." Mother stopped dead and said, "What was that? Was that English?" Father said, "The man's name is Terwilliger. He bunted." Mother thought that was terrific. For the next ten or twelve years she made this surprising string of syllables her own. If she was testing a microphone, or if she was pretending to whisper a secret in my ear, she said, "Terwilliger bunts one." If she had ever had an occasion to create a motto for a coat of arms, as Andrew Carnegie had, her motto would have been "Terwilliger bunts one." Carnegie's was "Death to privilege."

These fine parents taught my sisters and me moral courage, insofar as we have it, and tolerance, and how to dance all night without dragging your arms on your partner, and how to time the telling of a joke.

I've learned a lot by writing this book, not only about writing but about American history. Eastern woodland

Indians killed many more settlers than plains Indians did. By the time settlers made it to Sioux and Apache country those Indians had been so weakened by disease and by battles with the army that they didn't have much fight left in them. It was the settlers in the Pennsylvania forests and in Maryland and Virginia who kept getting massacred and burned out and taken captive and tortured. During the four years the French held Pittsburgh at Fort Duquesne they armed the Indians and sent them out from there, raiding and killing English-speaking settlers. These were mostly Scotch-Irish, because the Penn family let them settle in Pennsylvania only if they would serve as a "buffer sect" between Quakers and Indians. When the English held Pittsburgh at Fort Pitt they gave the Indians unwashed blankets from the smallpox hospital.

I put in early industry, because it was unexpectedly interesting. Before there was steel, everything was made out of wrought iron—which I find just amazing. Railroad ties were made out of wrought iron, as if they were candle sconces. Men had to carry wrought iron railroad ties all up and down the country. Wrought iron is made by iron puddlers, who belong to the iron puddlers' union, the Sons of Vulcan. It's a very difficult process: you stir slag back into iron, and it requires skilled labor because carbon monoxide bubbles up. The language is also nice. To sinter, for instance, is to convert flu dust to clinker. And I finally learned what coke is. When I was a child I thought that Coca-Cola was a by-product of steelmaking.

I learned about the heyday of the big industrialists and the endless paradox of Andrew Carnegie, the only one of the great American moguls who not only read books but actually wrote them, including one with a very American title, *The Gospel of Wealth*. He sold U.S. Steel to J. P. Morgan for $492 million, and he said, "A man who dies rich dies disgraced." He gave away ninety percent of his fortune in the few years he had left. While he was giving away money, many people were moved, understandably, to write him letters. He got one such letter from his friend Mark Twain. It said:

> You seem to be in prosperity. Could you lend an admirer a dollar & a half to buy a hymn-book with? God will bless you. I feel it. I know it.
> P.S. Don't send the hymn-book, send the money.

Carnegie was only five feet three inches tall. He weighed 133 pounds. He built the workers free libraries and museums and an art gallery at the same time that he had them working sixteen hours a day, six days a week, at subhuman wages, and drinking water full of typhoid and cholera because he and the other business owners opposed municipal works like water filtration plants. By 1906 Pittsburgh had the highest death rate in the nation because of wretched living conditions, and yet it was the seat of "wealth beyond computation, wealth beyond imagination." People built stables for their horses with gold mirrors in the stalls. The old Scotch-Irish families were horrified at the new millionaires who popped up around this time because they liked things pretty quiet. One new millionaire went to a barber on Penn Avenue for his first shampoo and the barber reported that the washing brought out "two ounces of fine Mesabi ore and a scattering of slag and cinders."

And what to leave out?

Well, I'm not writing social history. This is not one of those books in which you may read the lyrics or even the titles of popular songs on the radio. Or the names of radio and TV programs, or advertising slogans or product names or clothing fashions. I don't like all that. I want to direct the reader's attention in equal parts to the text—as a formal object—and to the world, as an interesting place in which we find ourselves.

So another thing I left out, as far as I could, was myself. The personal pronoun can be the subject of the verb: "I see this, I did that." But not the object of the verb: "I analyze me, I discuss me, I describe me, I quote me."

In the course of writing this memoir I've learned all

sorts of things, quite inadvertently, about myself and various relationships. But these things are not important to the book and I easily leave them out. Since the subject of the book is not me, other omissions naturally follow. I leave out many things that were important to my life but of no concern for the present book, like the summer I spent in Wyoming when I was fifteen. I keep the action in Pittsburgh; I see no reason to drag everybody off to Wyoming just because I want to tell them about my summer vacation. You have to take pains in a memoir not to hang on the reader's arm, like a drunk, and say, "And then I did this and it was so interesting." I don't write for that reason.

On the other hand, I dig deeply into the exuberant heart of a child and the restless, violent heart of an adolescent—and I was that child and I was that adolescent.

I leave out my private involvement with various young men. I didn't want to kiss and tell. I did put in several sections, however, about boys in general and the fascination they exerted. I ran around with one crowd of older boys so decadent, so accustomed to the most glittering of social lives, that one of them carried with him at all times, in his jacket pocket, a canister of dance wax so that he could be ready for anything. Other boys carry Swiss Army knives for those occasions which occur unexpectedly; this boy carried dance wax for the same reason. He could just sprinkle it on the dining room floor and take you in his arms and whirl you away. These were the sort of boys I knew; they had worn ties from the moment their mothers could locate their necks.

I tried to leave out anything that might trouble my family. My parents are quite young. My sisters are watching this book carefully. Everybody I'm writing about is alive and well, in full possession of his faculties, and possibly willing to sue. Things were simpler when I wrote about muskrats.

Writing in the first person can trap the writer into airing grievances. When I taught writing I spent a lot of time trying to convince young writers that, while literature is an art, it's not a martial art—that the pages of a short story or a novel are no place to defend yourself from an attack, real or imagined, and no place from which to launch an attack, particularly an attack against the very people who painstakingly reared you to your present omniscience.

I have no temptation to air grievances; in fact, I have no grievances left. Unfortunately, I seem to have written the story of my impassioned adolescence so convincingly that my parents (after reading that section of my book) think I still feel that way. It's a problem that I have to solve—one of many in this delicate area. My parents and my youngest sister still live in Pittsburgh; I have to handle it with tongs.

As a result of all of this, I've promised my family that

each may pass on the book. I've promised to take out anything that anyone objects to—anything at all. When I was growing up I didn't really take to Pittsburgh society, and I was happy to throw myself into any other world I could find. But I guess I can't say so, because my family may think that I confuse them with conventional Pittsburgh society people in the '50s.

I know a writer who cruelly sticks his parents into all his short stories and still pleases them both, because his mother is pleased to see his father look bad and his father is pleased to see his mother look bad. I had, I thought, nothing but good to say about all named people, but I'll make all that better yet. I don't believe in a writer's kicking around people who don't have access to a printing press. They can't defend themselves.

My advice to memoir writers is to embark upon a memoir for the same reason that you would embark on any other book: to fashion a text. Don't hope in a memoir to preserve your memories. If you prize your memories as they are, by all means avoid—eschew— writing a memoir. Because it is a certain way to lose them. You can't put together a memoir without cannibalizing your own life for parts. The work battens on your memories. And it replaces them.

It's a matter of writing's vividness for the writer. If you spend a couple of days writing a tricky paragraph, and if you spend a week or two laying out a scene or describing an event, you've spent more time writing about it than you did living it. The writing time is also much more intense.

After you've written, you can no longer remember anything but the writing. However true you make that writing, you've created a monster. This has happened to me many, many times, because I'm willing to turn events into pieces of paper. After I've written about any experience, my memories—those elusive, fragmentary patches of color and feeling—are gone; they've been replaced by the work. The work is a sort of changeling on the doorstep—not your baby but someone else's baby rather like it, different in some way that you can't pinpoint, and yours has vanished.

Memory is insubstantial. Things keep replacing it. Your batch of snapshots will both fix and ruin your memory of your travels, or your childhood, or your children's childhood. You can't remember anything from your trip except this wretched collection of snapshots. The painting you did of the light on the water will forever alter the way you see the light on the water; so will looking at Flemish paintings. If you describe a dream you'll notice that at the end of the verbal description you've lost the dream but gained a verbal description. You have to like verbal descriptions a lot to keep up this sort of thing. I like verbal descriptions a lot.

Let me put in a word now for a misunderstood genre: literary nonfiction. It's interesting to me because I try to write it and because I respect the art of it very much.

I like to be aware of a book as a piece of writing, and aware of its structure as a product of mind, and yet I want to be able to see the represented world through it. I admire artists who succeed in dividing my attention more or less evenly between the world of their books and the art of their books. In fiction we might say that the masters are Henry James and Herman Melville. In nonfiction the writer usually just points to the world and says, "This is a biography of Abraham Lincoln. This is what Abraham Lincoln was about." But the writer may also make of his work an original object in its own right, so that a reader may study the work with pleasure as well as the world that it describes. That is, works of nonfiction can be coherent and crafted works of literature.

It's not simply that they're carefully written, or vivid and serious and pleasing, like Boswell's *Life of Johnson*, say, or St. Exupéry's wonderful memoir of early aviation, *Wind, Sand, and Stars.* It's not even that they may contain elements of fiction, that their action reveals itself in scenes that use visual descriptions and that often use dialogue. It's not just these things, although these things are important. It's that nonfiction accounts may be literary insofar as the parts of their structures cohere internally, insofar as the things are in them for the sake of the work itself, and insofar as the work itself exists in the service of idea. (It is especially helpful if the writer so fully expresses the idea in materials that only a trained technician can find it. Because the abstract structure of a given text, which is of great interest to the writer and serves to rouse him out of bed in the morning and impel him to the desk, is of little or no interest to the reader, and he'd better not forget it.)

Nonfiction accounts don't ordinarily meet these criteria, but they may. Walden Pond is the linchpin of a metaphysic. In repeated and self-conscious rewritings Thoreau hammered at its unremarkable and rather dreary acres until they fastened eternity in time and stood for the notion that the physical world itself expresses a metaphysical one. He picked up that pond and ran with it. He could just as readily have used something else—a friend, say, or a chestnut. You can do quite a bit with language.

Hemingway in *Green Hills of Africa* wrote a sober narrative account of killing a kudu, the whole of which functions as an elaborate metaphor for internal quests and conquests. Loren Eiseley lays in narrative symbols with a trowel, splashing mortar all over the place, but they hold. In his essay "The Star-Thrower," Eiseley's beachcomber who throws dying starfish back into the surf stands for any hope or mercy that flies in the face of harsh natural law. He stands finally for the extravagant spirit behind creation as a whole; he is a god hurling solar systems into the void.

I only want to remind my writing colleagues that a great deal can be done in nonfiction, especially in first-person accounts where the writer controls the materials absolutely. Because other literary genres are shrinking. Poetry has purified itself right out of the ballpark. Literary fiction is scarcely being published—it's getting to be like conceptual art. All that the unknown writer of fiction can do is to tell his friends about the book he has written, and all that his friends can say is "Good idea." The short story is to some extent going the way of poetry, limiting its subject matter to such narrow surfaces that it can't handle the things that most engage our hearts and minds. But literary nonfiction is all over the map and has been for three hundred years. There's nothing you can't do with it. No subject matter is forbidden, no structure is proscribed. You get to make up your own form every time.

When I gave up writing poetry I was very sad, for I had devoted fifteen years to the study of how the structures of poems carry meaning. But I was delighted to find that nonfiction prose can also carry meaning in its structures and, like poetry, can tolerate all sorts of figurative language, as well as alliteration and even rhyme. The range of rhythms in prose is larger and grander than it is in poetry, and it can handle discursive ideas and plain information as well as character and story. It can do everything. I felt as though I had switched from a single reed instrument to a full orchestra.

Let me close with a word about process. There's a common notion that self-discipline is a freakish peculiarity of writers—that writers differ from other people by possessing enormous and equal portions of talent and willpower. They grit their powerful teeth and go into their little rooms. I think that's a bad misunderstanding of what impels the writer. What impels the writer is a deep love for and respect for language, for literary forms, for books. It's a privilege to muck about in sentences all morning. It's a challenge to bring off a powerful effect, or to tell the truth about something. You don't do it from willpower; you do it from an abiding passion for the field. I'm sure it's the same in every other field.

Writing a book is like rearing children—willpower has very little to do with it. If you have a little baby crying in the middle of the night, and if you depend only on willpower to get you out of bed to feed the baby, that baby will starve. You do it out of love. Willpower is a weak idea; love is strong. You don't have to scourge yourself with a cat-o'-nine-tails to go to the baby. You go to the baby out of love for that particular baby. That's the same way you go to your desk. There's nothing freakish about it. Caring passionately about something isn't against nature, and it isn't against human nature. It's what we're here to do.

ALFRED KAZIN

The Past Breaks Out

A Walker in the City, published in 1951 as a sensory memory of boyhood in the Brownsville district of Brooklyn, began as something else. When the war, Hitler's war, was over, I returned from wartime reporting in England to find that there was no room for me in New York except in a ramshackle painter's studio on Pineapple Street in Brooklyn Heights, indifferently left to me when the painter moved on to big money in commercial art. He even left me his old paintings, which consisted of violently colored images, a whole series of concentration camp prisoners standing with clenched fists behind barbed wire.

The house itself had seen better days. The greasy, spattered front steps, just off the Chinese hand laundry in the basement, led into what must have been the vestibule of a traditionally stately Brooklyn Heights mansion. Despite the metal shields holding up the battered front door, you could see that it had once been a beautiful door, like the many beautiful doors of grand old brownstones still lining Columbia Heights, Hicks Street and the other streets veering toward the harbor and Brooklyn Bridge.

Pineapple Street, just off Fulton, was in a poor way just then, and so was I. Across the street, just above the garbage cans put out by the local coffeeshop, hung the lopsided bronze plaque put up by the Authors League commemorating the exact site where in 1851 Walt Whitman himself helped put *Leaves of Grass* into type. Whenever I went up to my top floor studio I could smell the remains of some ancient smoke. There had once been a fire. The building still smelled of fire. My two rooms on the top floor had obviously been cut out of something larger, and despite the makeshift wall between the Puerto Rican carpenter next door and myself, he woke me every morning when Pineapple Street was still dark just by the racket he made on the other side of the wall getting himself ready to leave for work.

I would lie in bed listening to tugs hooting three blocks away; the harbor was all around me, and, when it rained, my painter's great north windows were awash with foggy sea light. The floors went every which way, but there was a skylight; the place was full of light. The evenings were lonely and even a little terrible as I lay on a couch in the other room staring at the violently colored concentration camp prisoners, grim behind barbed wire. I had no respect for these paintings, but would not take them down.

Much as I had always loved the neighboring streets and walking the promenade below Columbia Heights, with its full view of *the* bridge of bridges and the port of New York, I was unsure of everything else. A moment had come into my life, as can happen to men after thirty, when only the opening of Dante's *Inferno* spoke to my condition: "In the middle of our life, I found myself in a dark wood, for the straight way was lost."

A marriage had broken down during the war; I had not recovered. Hitler and his war had come to an end; it would never be over for me. On April 15, 1945, when I was still reporting political discussion groups in the British Army, a British detachment in the north of Germany had stumbled on the deeply hidden Belsen concentration camp in the vicinity of Hanover to find typhus raging, forty thousand sick, starving, dying prisoners, thirteen thousand corpses stacked on the ground. The London *Times* carried a dispatch from a correspondent with the army unit: "I have something to report that lies beyond the imagination of mankind." A week or so later, waiting out in the rain in the entrance to a music store, I heard a radio playing into the street the first Sabbath service from Belsen. When the liberated Jewish prisoners in unison recited the *Shema* —"Hear, O Israel, the Lord Our God, the Lord Is One"—I felt myself carried back to the old Friday evenings at home, when with the Sabbath at sundown a healing quietness would come over Brownsville.

In Pineapple Street, surrounded by New York and the harbor through which my parents as young rebels still unknown to each other had entered the country, I dreamed of putting my life in order by writing a book set against the New York background. This was no great departure from the criticism I had been writing for years. Criticism for me was not a theory, least of all a theory holding academics together. It was a branch of literature, a way of writing like any other—of characterization, analysis and almost physical empathy. Far from feeling confined to one mode of writing, I had been keeping all my life, since boyhood, a voluminous daily journal, or sketchbook, into which went everything that I felt like describing and thinking about.

What I liked most about this intimate record was writing in it, first thing every morning, in complete spontaneity and naturalness, lifelike and at the quick, as the French say. It represented some effort to think my life out. It also got me away from editors and their subjective dogmas about the public taste and capacity; this, at least, was all for myself. At the same time it was a cherished connection with something fundamental to American literature—the writing of personal history: diaries, journals, letters, memoirs. The influence of Puritanism had created a habit of mind that had persisted into the "American Renaissance" and the peculiarly personal reverberations in Emerson, Thoreau, Whitman and how many others—the need to present to God, the Eternal Reader and Judge of the soul's pilgrimage on earth, the veritable record of one's inner life.

At fourteen or fifteen my fascination with autobiography as narrative had accelerated when *The Education of Henry Adams* went on sale at the Abraham and Straus department store on Fulton Street in downtown Brooklyn. Without being able to say why, I knew that this particular book was more for me than the other book on sale, *The Autobiography of Benvenuto Cellini*.

There was something odd and even comic about what was to develop into a lifelong passion for everything to do with the Adamses. I was the first native child of Russian Jews, lived in the mostly Jewish (now mostly black) Brownsville district near the end of the I.R.T. subway, a notoriously rough, tough neighborhood trailing out into haunts of the Mafia. If my mother had known the sour opinions of Jews developed by the violently disillusioned patrician Henry Adams, the grandson and great-grandson of presidents, the most brilliant descendant of the most gifted American political family, she would have thrown *The Education of Henry Adams* out of the house—and me right after it.

But my mother didn't read English; she didn't read anything. It might have been interesting to inform my mother that Henry Adams's great-grandmother Abigail had written to her husband John during the Battle of Bunker Hill, "The race is not to the swift, nor the battle to the strong, but the God of Israel is He that giveth strength and power unto His people. Trust in Him at all times, ye people pour out your hearts before Him. God is a refuge for me—Charlestown is laid in ashes." After the Civil War, when the race *was* to the swift, Henry Adams felt himself so out of it that he likened himself to a Jew. "Had he been born in Jerusalem under the shadow of the Temple, and circumcised in the Synagogue by his uncle the high priest, under the name of Israel Cohen, he would scarcely have been more distinctly branded, and not much more heavily handicapped in the races of the coming century."

There was never a chance to go into such interesting items of American history with my mother—to explain why Henry Adams so came to associate capitalism with Jews that he habitually referred to J. P. Morgan as a Jew. My mother lived apart from such intellectual hatreds. She had come to America as a young seamstress because she believed herself to be unmarriageable, a plain girl in a family where a good-looking sister, named Shana ("Beautiful"), was the favorite. To remain unmarried was unthinkable for a good Jewish girl.

In America my mother found my father-to-be. That, so to speak, was the limit of her acquaintance with the country. But getting to America did save my mother's life; Shana and her husband were to be horribly killed by the Nazis in a roundup of their village. In any event, my mother's America, though not extensive, was certainly intense. It consisted of her family alive in America, dead or dying in Russia, and the sewing machine in our kitchen, where as a "home" dressmaker she kept my sister and me in college during the Depression when my father, a housepainter, could find occasional day jobs only when the New Deal shelled out for the painting of subway stations and bridges.

My debt to *The Education of Henry Adams* and other "personal" American classics—the essays and journals of Emerson; *Walden* and the journals of Thoreau especially; *Leaves of Grass* and Whitman's diary of the Civil War, *Specimen Days*—is simply stated. One could be a writer without writing a novel. Every taxi driver and bartender who told you his story wanted to be a novelist. It was the expected, the Big Thing, in America especially; it had raised to the heights literary prima donnas from Mark Twain to Norman Mailer. It seemed positively perverse to Leslie Fiedler, when he reviewed my *A Walker in the City,* that the book "obstinately refuses to become a novel."

At the moment, however, waking up uneasily every morning in Pineapple Street to the glare of postwar New York, so different from the Depression '30s and my early working-class life in Brownsville, I was trying to write something about the city at large that would do justice to the color, the variety, the imperial range I encountered walking about the city every day. Every next day I tried to get into my notebook what Whitman in his greatest New York poem, "Crossing Brooklyn Ferry," had called "the glories strung like beads on my smallest sights and hearings—on the walk in the street, and the passage over the river."

There was some connection I had to establish between writing and roaming the city, between writing and my ability to react to everything in the open street. To my delight and everlasting gratitude, I was assigned by *Harper's Bazaar* to work with the photographer Henri Cartier-Bresson on a piece about the Brooklyn Bridge and the different worlds at each end of it. I was later to describe this great artist as an aristocratic radical; he was gently disdainful of the new mass housing projects crowding the view of the Lower East Side from the Brooklyn Bridge—many of them named after

labor and Socialist heroes my father worshiped. But old
New York, still visible in the late '40s, gave particular
pleasure to Cartier-Bresson's genius eye as we walked
the wooden boardwalk down the center of the bridge.

"It breathes!" Cartier-Bresson said happily about this
central promenade. "See how it breathes!" With his
devastating clarity and my zeal for those leftover streets
we brought home the Brooklyn Bridge still anchored
in the iron age, the "Swamp" district of leather facto-
ries, old assayers' shops, dealers in perfumes and wines,
the ornamental fire escapes still sculptured with John
L. Sullivan prize-fighter figures out of the old *Police
Gazette*. Cartier-Bresson and I got on so well that we
thought of doing *tout New York* in a book. But this
never worked out, and I soon began writing such a
book on my own.

It was very ambitious, a sort of personal epic all
around New York, like *Leaves of Grass* and Hart
Crane's *The Bridge*, in prose. In the first section I tried
to cover morning in Pineapple Street, the blaze of midtown at noon and in the rush hour, the crowds, the
museums, the libraries. The third section was all about
Sunday in New York, full of color, poignance and
what I thought was dazzling prose. The middle section,
called "The Old Neighborhood," consisted of some
dozen pages of childhood memories, which I had written in a strange burst of enthusiasm in just one after-

noon but which didn't seem grand enough as a subject by comparison with midtown at noon and the city on Sunday.

What I went through for an absurdly long time trying to hammer the thing together does not deserve extended description here. But how I tried! I was a critic with a critic's weakness for ideas, and all I had then was a critic's ideas. Finally, after a ridiculously long time, I realized that I was not going to write a personal epic like *Leaves of Grass* or *The Bridge* or *Paterson* or any other of the "Columbiads" that ever since the eighteenth-century Joel Barlow have tempted our would-be Homers and Virgils. Carlyle sneered that Whitman thought he was a big poet because he lived in a big country. I suddenly opted for a small country, my natal country. The only thing emotionally authentic in my vast manuscript was those carelessly scribbled pages about growing up in Brownsville. On these, once I realized just how sensory the material really was and how vivid the prose would have to be, I could build my book.

But Brownsville—"Brunzvil," as the newly prosperous Jews long removed from it still described it? It's true that the splendid art historian Meyer Schapiro had passed through it, along with various Nobel laureates, Danny Kaye and John Garfield in East New York next door, Murder Incorporated, the crazy neighborhood thieves I actually saw skipping from roof to roof just ahead of the cops. But Brownsville? Poor ghetto Brownsville? My parents still hung on for years after the war, poor as ever. My father, no doubt praying that the spirit of Eugene Debs would forgive him, timidly complained that non-union black painters were taking work away from him at lower rates. Brownsville was now so far behind the Jews, so far behind me, that after one particularly sad Friday evening supper with my parents I wrote in my notebook, "Every time I go back it all feels like a foreign country."

But when I came to write the actual book I began: "Every time I go back to Brownsville it is as if I had never been away." It was not behind me at all. When E. B. White removed to Maine from Manhattan he described himself as "homesick for loneliness." That was my case. As the past broke out in my book, it came to me more and more that there was no intellectual solution to my long search for the meaning of Jewishness. I would never fully fathom the hatred behind the Holocaust. I would never become pious in the orthodox Jewish fashion. I would never settle in a country that desired to be all-Jewish. I would never believe in socialism's "final conflict." I would certainly never ally myself with the financially and politically powerful or the born-again patriots who were picking up their ideologies from the ex-Left.

There was some enduring mystery, some metaphysical conundrum about being Jewish, that I was not likely to abandon. I could not get over the extraordinariness of Jewish persistence through the ages, its matter-of-fact continuity with itself, in all periods and places. The key was some heightened sense of existence, living the Jewish experience through and through. The basic fact, as my exact contemporary Saul Bellow had shown in his wonderful second book, *The Victim*, was the singularity for even a man of small gifts, in our increasingly suspicious and disenchanted world, of remaining a Jew, of remaining unsuspicious in one's deepest soul—unwearied.

Norman Mailer was to complain that the boy in *A Walker in the City* was too virtuous; Irving Howe that he did not correspond to the original facts; Lionel Trilling that the subject was a "schmo"; Oscar Handlin that there were not enough people in the book. All these Jewish sages were correct; the book astonished me, too, by going its own way. It was definitely not what anyone else would have written. But early on I realized that I was thinking in color, luxuriating in physical sensations. The breakthrough was stirring up from the depths some tangential, very slight, endlessly reverberatory memory of being taken to the old Brooklyn Children's Museum. Was it on Brooklyn Avenue?

The Children's Museum had some basic connection with my first sight of Audubon's prints of birds. The museum itself, as I followed its extensive filaments in memory, was a wooden construction vaguely reminiscent of some old American farmhouse already stamped in memory as standing alone on the prairie. When I was writing my favorite section of the book, "The Block and Beyond," on my earliest walks into the city "beyond" Brownsville itself, I found myself writing:

The day they took us to the Children's Museum—rain was dripping on the porch of that old wooden house, the halls lined with Audubon prints were hazel in the thin antique light—I was left with the distinct impression that I had been stirring between my fingers dried earth and fallen leaves that I found in between the red broken paving stones of some small American town.

From the beginning I wanted physical images, straight from the belly. In memory again—"It's memory," said Willa Cather, "the memory that goes with the vocation"—I step off the train at Rockaway Avenue, smell the leak out of the men's room, then the pickles from the stand just below the subway steps. In these opening pages I am eager to get all the contrary feelings involved in homecoming—"an instant rage comes over me, mixed with dread and some unexpected tenderness." This is still the end of the city, the faraway place that thought of everything else as "the city," making every journey into the city a grind. Only the very old seem to have been left:

It is always the old women in their shapeless flowered house-dresses and ritual wigs I see first; they give Brownsville back to me. In their soft dumpy bodies and the unbudging way they occupy the tenement stoops, their hands blankly folded in each other as if they had been sitting on these stoops from the beginning of time, I sense again the old foreboding that all my life would be like this.

I remember my mother's earliest complaint against me: "We are *urime yidn,* poor Jews. What do you want of us?"

But not forgetting or forgiving some early hopeless-ness, I am grabbed by the aliveness of the scene, the inextinguishable contrasts, the absurdity. There in the shadows of the El-darkened street is the torn flapping canvas sign still listing the boys who went to war, the stagnant wells of candy stores and pool parlors, the torches flaring at dusk over the vegetable stands and pushcarts, the neon-blazing fronts of liquor stores, the piles of halvah and chocolate kisses in the windows of the candy stores next to the *News* and *Mirror,* the dusty old drugstores where urns of rose and pink and blue colored water still swing from chains, and where next door Mr. A's sign still tells anyone walking down Rockaway Avenue that he has pants to fit any color suit.

These details now make me happy; the energy of the street, so much packed-up humanity, makes this tumultuously commercial street, all these automatic and violent transactions, something it is a pleasure to unravel, to make minute on paper.

In the last crazy afternoon light the neons over the delicatessens bathe all their wares in a cosmetic smile, but strip the street of every personal shadow and concealment. The torches over the pushcarts hold in a single breath of yellow flame the acid smell of half-sour pickles and herrings floating in their briny barrels. There is a dry rattle of loose newspaper sheets around the cracked stretched skins of the "chiney" oranges. Through the kitchen windows along every ground floor I can already see the containers of milk, the fresh round poppyseed evening rolls. Time for supper, time to go home.

On this last note I have found my rhythm, the push toward home and the pull away again, the longing for the secret treasure of family and Jewish togetherness, and the contrary motion of seeking the open treasure that is the great city, infinite New York that belonged not to "us" but to "them." A key to my book is of course this constant sense of division, even of flagrant contradiction between wanting the enclosure of home *and* the open city, both moral certainty and intellectual independence. This conflict has never ended for me, I confess, which may be one reason why, thirty-six years ago in Pineapple Street, I felt that I was at last discovering an inescapable truth about myself and no doubt about other Jews of my generation brought up on the old immigrant poverty and orthodoxy. To rebel against the tradition was somehow to hold fast to it.

To want it both ways was also to span a good deal of the vehemence of Jewish history in a way perhaps unimaginable just now to those children of suburbia for whom Jewishness is psychology and troubled self-defense. Or, wearing a chic inch of *yarmulke*, relishing the ballet and the nudes at the museum of art. For me, as for so many Jewish writers and intellectual troublemakers of a certain age and condition, life in the twentieth century has been essentially political—with Jews usually at every crux of our turbulent century.

When Captain Alfred Dreyfus was accused, on the basis of forgeries gleefully committed by ultra-rightists, of betraying French military secrets to imperial Germany, he was driven out of the army in the most humiliating public ceremony. The crowd looking on hooted and shrieked, "A bas les Juifs!" The future state of

Israel was in the mind of one observer in that crowd, Theodor Herzl. When Dr. Sigmund Freud in Vienna found himself virtually ostracized for his professional insights he proudly said, "Being a Jew, I knew I would be in the opposition." Leon Trotsky, Rosa Luxemburg, Gregory Zinoviev, Osip Mandelstam were confident that their being Jewish was historically insignificant; those who destroyed them did not think it insignificant. Replacing nineteenth-century illusions that the "Jewish question" would disappear under socialism, the twentieth century everywhere has seen the persecution and even the extermination of Jews wherever the state has total control. The crowd that cheered Dreyfus's disgrace was replaced by the crowd in occupied Warsaw cheering as Jews locked into the ghetto flung themselves out of windows to escape deportation.

A child of poor Russian Jews living a commonplace life in Brooklyn nevertheless feasted on every scrap of Russian memory. But beyond my innocent, literary associations with a Russian life that my parents had not really experienced themselves—imagine not speaking the language of the country you were born in!—my real passion was hearing tales of the early American West from my father. As a young immigrant painting boxcars on the Union Pacific Railroad he had gone all the way to Omaha, had heard his beloved Debs making fools of Bryan and Taft in the 1908 campaign, had been offered a homestead in Nebraska!

"Omaha" was the most beautiful word I had ever heard. "Homestead" was almost as beautiful. I could never forgive my father for not having taken that homestead.

"What would I have done there? I'm no farmer."

"You should have taken it! Why do we always live here!"

"It would have been unnatural," he wound up. "Nobody I knew."

"What a chance!"

"Don't be childish. Nobody I knew."

"Why? Why?"

"What do you want of us poor Jews?"

Under the cover of those Friday evenings, when I was about eleven, my favorite book was *The Boy's Life of Theodore Roosevelt.* Year by year T.R., the only American president born in New York City, became ever more my hero—the police commissioner who identified with a stray Jewish policeman as "straight New York," the historian and author, the only New York politician in history who could write an essay on "Dante in the Bowery." He was my guide to that other New York, the New York of Herman Melville, Henry James, Edith Wharton, Frederick Law Olmsted, Alfred Stieglitz—the New York to be achieved, in Whit-

man's words, by "the passage over the river." This was
a New York that began at the Battery, the old Aquar-
ium that had first been Castle Clinton, then Castle Garden, which before it became the immigrant receiving
station had been the opera house where Whitman had
been intoxicated by Italian sopranos.

"Beyond," as I wrote, "was anything old and American—the name *Fraunces Tavern* repeated to us on a
school excursion; the eighteenth-century muskets and
glazed oil paintings on the wall; the very streets, the
deeper you got into Brooklyn, named after generals of
the Revolutionary War—Putnam, Gates, Kosciusko,
DeKalb, Lafayette, Pulaski." "Beyond" was my discovery in the Brooklyn Museum of "a circular room
upstairs violently ablaze with John Singer Sargent's
watercolors of the Caribbean" and a long room lined
with dim farmscapes of old Brooklyn itself in the early
nineteenth century. "And I knew I would come back,
that I would have to come back."

The more I got into my book, the happier I became
getting back into the Metropolitan Museum, into the
old American Wing (not so lavishly laid out as it is
now). Far in the back, in an alcove near the freight
elevator, hung so low and the figures so dim in the faint
light that I crouched to take them in, were pictures of
New York sometime after the Civil War. Skaters in
Central Park, a red muffler flying in the wind; a gay

crowd moving round and round Union Square Park; horsecars charging between the brownstones of lower Fifth Avenue at dusk. I couldn't believe my eyes. Room on room they had painted my city, and this city was my country: Winslow Homer's dark oblong of Union soldiers making camp in the rain, tenting tonight, tenting on the old campground, as I had never thought I would get to see them when we sang that song in school; Thomas Eakins's solitary sculler on the Schuylkill, resting to have his portrait painted in the yellow light bright with patches of raw spring in Pennsylvania showing on the other side of him. Most wonderful to me then was John Sloan's picture of a young girl standing in the wind on the deck of a New York ferryboat —surely to Staten Island, and just about the year of my birth?—looking out to water.

America between the Civil War and the "Great War" was to become my favorite period for study. When I eventually discovered Lewis Mumford's *The Brown Decades,* a prime book on the subject, with its loving portraits of Emily Dickinson, John August Roebling, the creator of Brooklyn Bridge, and the painter Albert Pinkham Ryder (in those days you could still see on University Place the Hotel Albert, named after the mystical painter by his brother), I was hooked for life. It had everything to do with such historical items as Park Row on a winter afternoon in the 1880s, the snow falling into the dark stone streets under the Brooklyn Bridge, newsboys running under the maze of telegraph wires that darkened every street of the lower city. How those wires haunted me in every photograph I found of old New York. Indescribably heavy, they sagged between the poles; the very streets seemed to sink under their weight. The past was that forest of wires hung over lower New York at five o'clock.

Ever more vivid to me as the years went on were certain prime figures moving against that dark, brooding landscape: Melville the customs inspector checking cargoes on newly arrived ships all along the Hudson up to Harlem, bitter at the ignoramuses who didn't know that Gansevoort Street, where Melville took his lunch, was named after his own grandfather, the Revolutionary War hero. Later, seeing the ghosts of New York writers in *their* old neighborhoods, it was easy to imagine Mark Twain still living at Tenth Street and Fifth Avenue, more picturesque than anyone else as, with silk hat perched on his snowy white hair (washed every morning with laundry soap), he walked up Fifth Avenue just ahead of the crowd that always recognized and followed him. And finally, joining one past to another, there was Henry James on his native's return to the Lower East Side of New York in 1905, studying the fire escapes heaped with Jewish immigrants just like my father and mother. He would describe them all in that most majestic of travel books, *The American Scene.* But unlike me he would see them only in the mass, as faintly repellent intruders, agents of "future ravage."

All this did not complete the circle of memories; my forays into the past continued with *Starting Out in the Thirties* and *New York Jew.* Now, past seventy, I am still trying to make a book out of my lifetime notebooks called *Too Much Happens.* Mrs. Hines, Joe Christmas's grandmother in Faulkner's *Light in August,* muses after his death: "It is because so much happens. Too much happens." What happens every day, virtually every moment, can be an amazement still that I have to put down in writing. Let the future decipher it. My involvement with so much personal history has this excuse: it is about someone taken up in history, someone who was in history—like all his people—before he was born. And I cannot fully explain the necessity, which can be more unnerving to me than to the people I write about. But recently there was a moment when I felt repaid for all my struggles.

A Walker in the City is much used in composition courses, and while I was still teaching at Hunter College I was asked by some freshman students to answer questions about the book. A black girl said to me, a little angrily: "I come from Amboy and Sutter. I sure know the place. Teach me to write like that."

TONI MORRISON

The Site of Memory

My inclusion in a series of talks on autobiography and memoir is not entirely a misalliance. Although it's probably true that a fiction writer thinks of his or her work as alien in that company, what I have to say may suggest why I'm not completely out of place here. For one thing, I might throw into relief the differences between self-recollection (memoir) and fiction, and also some of the similarities—the places where those two crafts embrace and where that embrace is symbiotic.

But the authenticity of my presence here lies in the fact that a very large part of my own literary heritage is the autobiography. In this country the print origins of black literature (as distinguished from the oral origins) were slave narratives. These book-length narratives (autobiographies, recollections, memoirs), of which well over a hundred were published, are familiar texts to historians and students of black history. They range from the adventure-packed life of Olaudah Equiano's *The Interesting Narrative of the Life of Olaudah Equiano, or Gustavus Vassa, the African, Written by Himself* (1769) to the quiet desperation of *Incidents in the Life of a Slave Girl: Written by Herself* (1861), in which Harriet Jacob ("Linda Brent") records hiding for seven years in a room too small to stand up in; from the political savvy of Frederick Douglass's *Narrative of the Life of Frederick Douglass, an American Slave, Written by Himself* (1845) to the subtlety and modesty of Henry Bibb, whose voice, in *Life and Adventures of Henry Bibb, an American Slave, Written by Himself* (1849), is surrounded by ("loaded with" is a better phrase) documents attesting to its authenticity. Bibb is careful to note that his formal schooling (three weeks) was short, but that he was "educated in the school of adversity, whips, and chains." Born in Kentucky, he put aside his plans to escape in order to marry. But when he learned that he was the father of a slave and watched the degradation of his wife and child, he reactivated those plans.

Whatever the style and circumstances of these narratives, they were written to say principally two things. One: "This is my historical life—my singular, special example that is personal, but that also represents the race." Two: "I write this text to persuade other people —you, the reader, who is probably not black—that we are human beings worthy of God's grace and the immediate abandonment of slavery." With these two missions in mind, the narratives were clearly pointed.

In Equiano's account, the purpose is quite up-front. Born in 1745 near the Niger River and captured at the age of ten, he survived the Middle Passage, American plantation slavery, wars in Canada and the Mediterranean; learned navigation and clerking from a Quaker named Robert King, and bought his freedom at twenty-one. He lived as a free servant, traveling widely and living most of his latter life in England. Here he is speaking to the British without equivocation: "I hope to have the satisfaction of seeing the renovation of liberty and justice resting on the British government. . . . I hope and expect the attention of gentlemen of power. . . . May the time come—at least the speculation is to me pleasing—when the sable people shall gratefully commemorate the auspicious era of extensive freedom." With typically eighteenth-century reticence he records his singular and representative life for one purpose: to change things. In fact, he and his co-authors *did* change things. Their works gave fuel to the fires that abolitionists were setting everywhere.

More difficult was getting the fair appraisal of literary critics. The writings of church martyrs and confessors are and were read for the eloquence of their message as well as their experience of redemption, but the American slaves' autobiographical narratives were frequently scorned as "biased," "inflammatory" and "improbable." These attacks are particularly difficult to understand in view of the fact that it was extremely important, as you can imagine, for the writers of these narratives to appear as objective as possible—not to offend the reader by being too angry, or by showing too much outrage, or by calling the reader names. As recently as 1966, Paul Edwards, who edited and abridged Equiano's story, praises the narrative for its refusal to be "inflammatory."

"As a rule," Edwards writes, "he [Equiano] puts no emotional pressure on the reader other than that which the situation itself contains—his language does not strain after our sympathy, but expects it to be given naturally and at the proper time. This quiet avoidance of emotional display produces many of the best passages in the book." Similarly, an 1836 review of Charles Bell's *Life and Adventures of a Fugitive Slave,* which appeared in the "Quarterly Anti-Slavery Magazine," praised Bell's account for its objectivity. "We rejoice in the book the more, because it is not a partisan work. . . . It broaches no theory in regard to [slavery], nor proposes any mode or time of emancipation."

As determined as these black writers were to persuade the reader of the evil of slavery, they also complimented him by assuming his nobility of heart and his high-mindedness. They tried to summon up his finer nature in order to encourage him to employ it. They knew that their readers were the people who could make a difference in terminating slavery. Their stories —of brutality, adversity and deliverance—had great popularity in spite of critical hostility in many quarters and patronizing sympathy in others. There was a time when the hunger for "slave stories" was difficult to quiet, as sales figures show. Douglass's *Narrative* sold five thousand copies in four months; by 1847 it had sold eleven thousand copies. Equiano's book had thirty-six editions between 1789 and 1850. Moses Roper's book had ten editions from 1837 to 1856; William Wells Brown's was reprinted four times in its first year. Solomon Northrop's book sold twenty-seven thousand copies before two years had passed. A book by Josiah Henson (argued by some to be the model for the "Tom" of Harriet Beecher Stowe's *Uncle Tom's Cabin*) had a pre-publication sale of five thousand.

In addition to using their own lives to expose the horrors of slavery, they had a companion motive for their efforts. The prohibition against teaching a slave to read and write (which in many Southern states carried severe punishment) and against a slave's learning to read and write had to be scuttled at all costs. These writers knew that literacy was power. Voting, after all, was inextricably connected to the ability to read; literacy was a way of assuming and proving the "humanity" that the Constitution denied them. That is why the narratives carry the subtitle "written by himself," or "herself," and include introductions and prefaces by white sympathizers to authenticate them. Other narratives, "edited by" such well-known anti-slavery figures as Lydia Maria Child and John Greenleaf Whittier, contain prefaces to assure the reader how little editing was needed. A literate slave was supposed to be a contradiction in terms.

One has to remember that the climate in which they wrote reflected not only the Age of Enlightenment but its twin, born at the same time, the Age of Scientific Racism. David Hume, Immanuel Kant and Thomas Jefferson, to mention only a few, had documented their conclusions that blacks were incapable of intelligence. Frederick Douglass knew otherwise, and he wrote refutations of what Jefferson said in "Notes on the State of Virginia": "Never yet could I find that a black had uttered a thought above the level of plain narration, never see even an elementary trait of painting or sculpture." A sentence that I have always thought ought to be engraved at the door to the Rockefeller Collection of African Art. Hegel, in 1813, had said that Africans had no "history" and couldn't write in modern languages. Kant disregarded a perceptive observation by a black man by saying, "This fellow was quite black from head to foot, a clear proof that what he said was stupid."

Yet no slave society in the history of the world wrote more—or more thoughtfully—about its own enslavement. The milieu, however, dictated the purpose and the style. The narratives are instructive, moral and obviously representative. Some of them are patterned after the sentimental novel that was in vogue at the time. But whatever the level of eloquence or the form, popular taste discouraged the writers from dwelling too long or too carefully on the more sordid details of their experience. Whenever there was an unusually violent incident, or a scatological one, or something "excessive," one finds the writer taking refuge in the literary conventions of the day. "I was left in a state of distraction not to be described" (Equiano). "But let us now leave the rough usage of the field . . . and turn our attention to the less repulsive slave life as it existed in the house of my childhood" (Douglass). "I am not about to harrow the feelings of my readers by a terrific representation of the untold horrors of that fearful system of oppression. . . . It is not my purpose to descend deeply into the dark and noisome caverns of the hell of slavery" (Henry Box Brown).

Over and over, the writers pull the narrative up short

with a phrase such as, "But let us drop a veil over these proceedings too terrible to relate." In shaping the experience to make it palatable to those who were in a position to alleviate it, they were silent about many things, and they "forgot" many other things. There was a careful selection of the instances that they would record and a careful rendering of those that they chose to describe. Lydia Maria Child identified the problem in her introduction to "Linda Brent's" tale of sexual abuse: "I am well aware that many will accuse me of indecorum for presenting these pages to the public; for the experiences of this intelligent and much-injured woman belong to a class which some call delicate subjects, and others indelicate. This peculiar phase of Slavery has generally been kept veiled; but the public ought to be made acquainted with its monstrous features, and I am willing to take the responsibility of presenting them with the veil drawn [aside]."

But most importantly—at least for me—there was no mention of their interior life.

For me—a writer in the last quarter of the twentieth century, not much more than a hundred years after Emancipation, a writer who is black and a woman—the exercise is very different. My job becomes how to rip that veil drawn over "proceedings too terrible to relate." The exercise is also critical for any person who is black, or who belongs to any marginalized category, for, historically, we were seldom invited to participate in the discourse even when we were its topic.

Moving that veil aside requires, therefore, certain things. First of all, I must trust my own recollections. I must also depend on the recollections of others. Thus memory weighs heavily in what I write, in how I begin and in what I find to be significant. Zora Neale Hurston said, "Like the dead-seeming cold rocks, I have memories within that came out of the material that went to make me." These "memories within" are the subsoil of my work. But memories and recollections won't give me total access to the unwritten interior life of these people. Only the act of the imagination can help me.

If writing is thinking and discovery and selection and order and meaning, it is also awe and reverence and mystery and magic. I suppose I could dispense with the last four if I were not so deadly serious about fidelity to the milieu out of which I write and in which my ancestors actually lived. Infidelity to that milieu—the absence of the interior life, the deliberate excising of it from the records that the slaves themselves told—is precisely the problem in the discourse that proceeded without us. How I gain access to that interior life is what drives me and is the part of this talk which both distinguishes my fiction from autobiographical strategies and which also embraces certain autobiographical strategies. It's a kind of literary archeology: on the basis of some information and a little bit of guesswork you journey to a site to see what remains were left behind and to reconstruct the world that these remains imply. What makes it fiction is the nature of the imaginative act: my reliance on the image—on the remains—in addition to recollection, to yield up a kind of a truth. By "image," of course, I don't mean "symbol"; I simply mean "picture" and the feelings that accompany the picture.

Fiction, by definition, is distinct from fact. Presumably it's the product of imagination—invention—and it claims the freedom to dispense with "what really happened," or where it really happened, or when it really happened, and nothing in it needs to be publicly verifiable, although much in it can be verified. By contrast, the scholarship of the biographer and the literary critic seems to us only trustworthy when the events of fiction can be traced to some publicly verifiable fact. It's the research of the "Oh, yes, this is where he or she got it from" school, which gets its own credibility from excavating the credibility of the sources of the imagination, not the nature of the imagination.

The work that I do frequently falls, in the minds of most people, into that realm of fiction called fantastic, or mythic, or magical, or unbelievable. I'm not comfortable with these labels. I consider that my single gravest responsibility (in spite of that magic) is not to lie. When I hear someone say, "Truth is stranger than fiction," I think that old chestnut is truer than we know, because it doesn't say that truth is truer than fiction; just that it's stranger, meaning that it's odd. It may be excessive, it may be more interesting, but the important thing is that it's random—and fiction is not random.

Therefore the crucial distinction for me is not the difference between fact and fiction, but the distinction between fact and truth. Because facts can exist without human intelligence, but truth cannot. So if I'm looking to find and expose a truth about the interior life of people who didn't write it (which doesn't mean that they didn't have it); if I'm trying to fill in the blanks that the slave narratives left—to part the veil that was so frequently drawn, to implement the stories that I heard—then the approach that's most productive and most trustworthy for me is the recollection that moves from the image to the text. Not from the text to the image.

Simone de Beauvoir, in *A Very Easy Death*, says, "I don't know why I was so shocked by my mother's death." When she heard her mother's name being called at the funeral by the priest, she says, "Emotion seized me by the throat. . . . 'Françoise de Beauvoir': the words brought her to life; they summed up her history, from birth to marriage to widowhood to the grave. Françoise de Beauvoir—that retiring woman, so rarely named, became an *important* person." The book becomes an exploration both into her own grief and into the images in which the grief lay buried.

Unlike Mme. de Beauvoir, Frederick Douglass asks the reader's patience for spending about half a page on the death of his grandmother—easily the most profound loss he had suffered—and he apologizes by saying, in effect, "It really was very important to me. I hope you aren't bored by my indulgence." He makes no attempt to explore that death: its images or its meaning. His narrative is as close to factual as he can make it, which leaves no room for subjective speculation. James Baldwin, on the other hand, in *Notes of a Native Son*, says, in recording his father's life and his own relationship to his father, "All of my father's Biblical texts and songs, which I had decided were meaningless, were ranged before me at his death like empty bottles, waiting to hold the meaning which life would give them for me." And then his text fills those bottles. Like Simone de Beauvoir, he moves from the event to the image that it left. My route is the reverse: the image comes first and tells me what the "memory" is about.

I can't tell you how I felt when my father died. But I was able to write *Song of Solomon* and imagine, not him, and not his specific interior life, but the world that he inhabited and the private or interior life of the people in it. And I can't tell you how I felt reading to my grandmother while she was turning over and over in her bed (because she was dying, and she was not comfortable), but I could try to reconstruct the world that she lived in. And I have suspected, more often than not, that I *know* more than she did, that I *know* more than my grandfather and my great-grandmother did, but I also know that I'm no wiser than they were. And whenever I have tried earnestly to diminish their vision and prove to myself that I know more, and when I have tried to speculate on their interior life and match it up with my own, I have been overwhelmed every time by the richness of theirs compared to my own. Like Frederick Douglass talking about his grandmother, and James Baldwin talking about his father, and Simone de Beauvoir talking about her mother, these people are my access to me; they are my entrance into my own interior life. Which is why the images that float around them—the remains, so to speak, at the archeological site—surface first, and they surface so vividly and so compellingly that I acknowledge them as my route to a reconstruction of a world, to an exploration of an interior life that was not written and to the revelation of a kind of truth.

So the nature of my research begins with something as ineffable and as flexible as a dimly recalled figure, the corner of a room, a voice. I began to write my second book, which was called *Sula,* because of my preoccupation with a picture of a woman and the way in which I heard her name pronounced. Her name was Hannah, and I think she was a friend of my mother's. I don't remember seeing her very much, but what I do remember is the color around her—a kind of violet, a suffusion of something violet—and her eyes, which appeared to be half closed. But what I remember most is how the women said her name: how they said "Hannah Peace" and smiled to themselves, and there was some secret about her that they knew, which they didn't talk about, at least not in my hearing, but it seemed *loaded* in the way in which they said her name. And I suspected that she was a little bit of an outlaw but that they approved in some way.

And then, thinking about their relationship to her and the way in which they talked about her, the way in which they articulated her name, made me think about friendship between women. What is it that they forgive each other for? And what it is that is unforgivable in the world of women. I don't want to know any more about Miss Hannah Peace, and I'm not going to ask my mother who she really was and what did she do and what were you laughing about and why were you smiling? Because my experience when I do this with my mother is so crushing: she will give you *the* most pedestrian information you ever heard, and I would like to keep all of my remains and my images intact in their mystery when I begin. Later I will get to the facts. That way I can explore two worlds—the actual and the possible.

What I want to do this evening is to track an image from picture to meaning to text—a journey which appears in the novel that I'm writing now, which is called *Beloved.*

I'm trying to write a particular kind of scene, and I see corn on the cob. To "see" corn on the cob doesn't mean that it suddenly hovers; it only means that it keeps coming back. And in trying to figure out "What is all this corn doing?" I discover what it *is* doing.

I see the house where I grew up in Lorain, Ohio. My parents had a garden some distance away from our house, and they didn't welcome me and my sister there, when we were young, because we were not able to distinguish between the things that they wanted to grow and the things that they didn't, so we were not able to hoe, or weed, until much later.

I see them walking, together, away from me. I'm looking at their backs and what they're carrying in their arms: their tools, and maybe a peck basket. Sometimes when they walk away from me they hold hands, and they go to this other place in the garden. They have to cross some railroad tracks to get there.

I also am aware that my mother and father sleep at odd hours because my father works many jobs and works at night. And these naps are times of pleasure for me and my sister because nobody's giving us chores, or telling us what to do, or nagging us in any way. In addition to which, there is some feeling of pleasure in them that I'm only vaguely aware of. They're very rested when they take these naps.

And later on in the summer we have an opportunity to eat corn, which is the one plant that I can distinguish from the others, and which is the harvest that I like the best; the others are the food that no child likes—the collards, the okra, the strong, violent vegetables that I would give a great deal for now. But I do like the corn because it's sweet, and because we all sit down to eat it, and it's finger food, and it's hot, and it's even good cold, and there are neighbors in, and there are uncles in, and it's easy, and it's nice.

The picture of the corn and the nimbus of emotion surrounding it became a powerful one in the manuscript I'm now completing.

Authors arrive at text and subtext in thousands of ways, learning each time they begin anew how to recognize a valuable idea and how to render the texture that accompanies, reveals or displays it to its best advantage. The process by which this is accomplished is endlessly fascinating to me. I have always thought that as an editor for twenty years I understood writers better than their most careful critics, because in examining the manuscript in each of its subsequent stages I knew the author's process, how his or her mind worked, what was effortless, what took time, where the "solution" to a problem came from. The end result—the book—was all that the critic had to go on.

Still, for me, that was the least important aspect of the work. Because, no matter how "fictional" the account of these writers, or how much it was a product of invention, the act of imagination is bound up with memory. You know, they straightened out the Mississippi River in places, to make room for houses and livable acreage. Occasionally the river floods these places. "Floods" is the word they use, but in fact it is not flooding; it is remembering. Remembering where it used to be. All water has a perfect memory and is forever trying to get back to where it was. Writers are like that: remembering where we were, what valley we ran through, what the banks were like, the light that was there and the route back to our original place. It is emotional memory—what the nerves and the skin remember as well as how it appeared. And a rush of imagination is our "flooding."

Along with personal recollection, the matrix of the

work I do is the wish to extend, fill in and complement slave autobiographical narratives. But only the matrix. What comes of all that is dictated by other concerns, not least among them the novel's own integrity. Still, like water, I remember where I was before I was "straightened out."

———

Q. I would like to ask about your point of view as a novelist. Is it a vision, or are you taking the part of the particular characters?

A. I try sometimes to have genuinely minor characters just walk through, like a walk-on actor. But I get easily distracted by them, because a novelist's imagination goes like that: every little road looks to me like an adventure, and once you begin to claim it and describe it, it looks like more, and you invent more and more and more. I don't mind doing that in my first draft, but afterward I have to cut back. I have seen myself get distracted, and people have loomed much larger than I had planned, and minor characters have seemed a little bit more interesting than they need to be for the purposes of the book. In that case I try to endow them: if there are little pieces of information that I want to reveal, I let them do some of the work. But I try not to get carried away; I try to restrain it, so that, finally, the texture is consistent and nothing is wasted; there are no words in the final text that are unnecessary, and no people who are not absolutely necessary.

As for the point of view, there should be the illusion that it's the characters' point of view, when in fact it isn't; it's really the narrator who is there but who doesn't make herself (in my case) known in that role. I like the feeling of a *told* story, where you hear a voice but you can't identify it, and you think it's your own voice. It's a comfortable voice, and it's a guiding voice, and it's alarmed by the same things that the reader is alarmed by, and it doesn't know what's going to happen next either. So you have this sort of guide. But that guide can't have a personality; it can only have a sound, and you have to feel comfortable with this voice, and then this voice can easily abandon itself and reveal the interior dialogue of a character. So it's a combination of using the point of view of various characters but still retaining the power to slide in and out, provided that when I'm "out" the reader doesn't see little fingers pointing to what's in the text.

What I really want is that intimacy in which the reader is under the impression that he isn't really reading this; that he is participating in it as he goes along. It's unfolding, and he's always two beats ahead of the characters and right on target.

Q. You have said that writing is a solitary activity. Do you go into steady seclusion when you're writing, so that your feelings are sort of contained, or do you have to get away, and go out shopping and . . . ?

A. I do all of it. I've been at this book for three years. I go out shopping, and I stare, and I do whatever. It goes away. Sometimes it's very intense and I walk—I mean, I write a sentence and I jump up and run outside or something; it sort of beats you up. And sometimes I don't. Sometimes I write long hours every day. I get up at 5:30 and just go do it, and if I don't like it the next day, I throw it away. But I sit down and do it. By now I know how to get to that place where something is working. I didn't always know; I thought every thought I had was interesting—because it was mine. Now I know better how to throw away things that are not useful. I can stand around and do other things and think about it at the same time. I don't mind not writing every minute; I'm not so terrified.

When you first start writing—and I think it's true for a lot of beginning writers—you're scared to death that if you don't get that sentence right that minute it's never going to show up again. And it isn't. But it doesn't matter—another one will, and it'll probably be better. And I don't mind writing badly for a couple of days because I know I can fix it—and fix it again and again and again, and it will be better. I don't have the hysteria that used to accompany some of those dazzling passages that I thought the world was just dying for me to remember. I'm a little more sanguine about it now. Because the best part of it all, the absolutely most delicious part, is finishing it and then doing it over. That's the thrill of a lifetime for me: if I can just get done with that first phase and then have infinite time to fix it and change it. I rewrite a lot, over and over again, so that it looks like I never did. I try to make it look like I never touched it, and that takes a lot of time and a lot of sweat.

Q. In "Song of Solomon," what was the relationship between your memories and what you made up? Was it very tenuous?

A. Yes, it was tenuous. For the first time I was writing a book in which the central stage was occupied by men, and which had something to do with my loss, or my perception of loss, of a man (my father) and the world that disappeared with him. (It didn't, but I *felt* that it did.) So I was re-creating a time period that was his—not biographically his life or anything in it; I use whatever's around. But it seemed to me that there was this big void after he died, and I filled it with a book that was about men because my two previous books had had women as the central characters. So in that sense it was about my memories and the need to invent. I had to do something. I was in such a rage because my father was dead. The connections between us were threads that I either mined for a lot of strength or they were purely invention. But I created a male world and inhabited it and it had this quest—a journey from stupidity to epiphany, of a man, a complete man. It was my way of exploring all that, of trying to figure out what he may have known.

LEWIS THOMAS

A Long Line of Cells

It should be easier, certainly shorter work to compose a memoir than an autobiography, and surely it is easier to sit and listen to the one than to the other. An autobiography, I take it, is a linear account of one thing after another, leading—progressively, one hopes—to one's personal state of affairs at the moment of writing. In my case this would run to over seventy years, one after the other, discounting maybe twenty-five of the seventy spent sleeping, leaving around forty-five to be dealt with. Even so, a lot of time to be covered if all the events were to be recalled and laid out.

But discount again the portion of those 16,500 days, 264,000 waking hours, spent doing not much of anything—reading the papers, staring at blank sheets of paper, walking from one room to the next, speaking a great deal of small talk and listening to still more, waiting around for the next thing to happen, whatever. Delete all this as irrelevant, then line up what's left in the proper linear order without fudging. There you are with an autobiography, now relieved of an easy three-fourths of the time lived, leaving only eleven years, or 4,000 days, or 64,000 hours. Not much to remember, but still too much to write down.

But now take out all the blurred memories, all the recollections you suspect may have been dressed up by your mind in your favor, leaving only the events you can't get out of your head, the notions that keep leaping to the top of your mind, the ideas you're stuck with, the images that won't come unstuck, including the ones you'd just as soon do without. Edit these down sharply enough to reduce 64,000 hours to around thirty minutes, and there's your memoir.

In my case, going down this shortened list of items, I find that most of what I've got left are not real memories of my own experience, but mainly the remembrances of other people's thoughts, things I've read or been told, metamemories. A surprising number turn out to be wishes rather than recollections, hopes that the place really did work the way everyone said it was supposed to work, hankerings that the one thing leading to another has a direction of some kind, and a hope for a pattern from the jumble—an epiphany out of entropy.

To begin personally on a confessional note, I was at one time, at my outset, a single cell. I have no memory of this stage of my life, but I know it to be true because everyone says so. There was of course a sort of half-life before that, literally half, when the two half-endowed, haploid gametes, each carrying half my chromosomes, were off on their own looking to bump into each other and did so, by random chance, sheer luck, for better or worse, richer or poorer, et cetera, and I got under way.

I do not remember this, but I know that I began dividing. I have probably never worked so hard, and never again with such skill and certainty. At a certain stage, very young, a matter of hours of youth, I sorted myself out and became a system of cells, each labeled for what it was to become—brain cells, limbs, liver, the lot—all of them signaling to each other, calculating their territories, laying me out. At one stage I possessed an excellent kidney, good enough for any higher fish; then I thought better and destroyed it all at once, installing in its place a neater pair for living on land. I didn't plan on this when it was going on, but my cells, with a better memory, did.

Thinking back, I count myself lucky that I was not in charge at the time. If it had been left to me to do the mapping of my cells I would have got it wrong, dropped something, forgotten where to assemble my neural crest, confused it. Or I might have been stopped in my tracks, panicked by the massive deaths, billions of my embryonic cells being killed off systematically to make room for their more senior successors, death on a scale so vast that I can't think of it without wincing. By the time I was born, more of me had died than survived. It is no wonder I can't remember; during that time I went through brain after brain for nine months, finally contriving the one model that could be human, equipped for language.

It is because of language that I am able now to think farther back into my lineage. By myself, I can only remember two parents, one grandmother and the family stories of Welshmen, back into the shadows when all the Welsh were kings, but no farther. From there on I must rely on reading the texts.

They instruct me that I go back to the first of my immediate line, the beginner, the earliest *Homo sapiens*, human all the way through, or not quite human if you measure humanness as I do by the property of language and *its* property, the consciousness of an indisputably singular, unique self. I'm not sure how far back that takes me, and no one has yet told me about this convincingly. When did my relations begin speaking?

Writing is easier to trace, having started not more than a few years back, maybe 10,000 years, not much more. Tracking speech requires guesswork. If we were slow learners, as slow as we seem to be in solving today's hard problems, my guess is that we didn't begin talking until sometime within the last 100,000 years, give or take 50,000. That is what's called a rough scientific guess. But no matter, it is an exceedingly short time ago, and I am embarrassed at the thought that so many of my ancestors, generations of them—all the way back to the very first ones a million-odd years ago —may have been speechless. I am modestly proud to have come from a family of tool makers, bone scratchers, grave diggers, cave painters. Humans all. But it hurts to think of them as so literally dumb, living out their lives without metaphors, deprived of conversation, even small talk. I would prefer to have had them arrive fully endowed, talking their heads off, the moment evolution provided them with braincases large enough to contain words, so to speak. But it was not so, I must guess, and language came late. I will come back to this matter.

What sticks in the top of my mind is another, unavoidable aspect of my genealogy, far beyond my memory, but remembered still, I suspect, by all my cells. It is a difficult and delicate fact to mention. To face it squarely, I come from a line that can be traced straight back, with some accuracy, into a near-infinity of years before my first humanoid ancestors turned up. I go back, and so do you, like it or not, to a single Urancestor whose remains are on display in rocks dated approximately 3.5 thousand million years ago, born a billion or so years after the earth itself took shape and began cooling down. That first of the line, our n-grand-uncle, was unmistakably a bacterial cell.

I cannot get this out of my head. It has become, for the moment, the most important thing I know, the obligatory beginning of any memoir, the long-buried source of language. We derive from a lineage of bacteria, and a very long line at that. Never mind our embarrassed indignation when we were first told, last century, that we came from a family of apes and had chimps as near-cousins. That was relatively easy to accommodate, having at least the distant look of a set of relatives. But this new connection, already fixed by recent science beyond any hope of disowning the parentage, is something else again. At first encounter the news must come as a kind of humiliation. Humble origins indeed.

But then, it is some comfort to acknowledge that we've had an etymological hunch about such an origin since the start of our language. Our word "human" comes from the Proto-Indo-European root *dhghem*, meaning simply "earth." The most telling cognate word is "humus," the primary product of microbial industry. Also, for what it's worth, "humble." Also "humane." It gives a new sort of English, in the sense of a strange spin, to the old cliché for an apology: "Sorry, I'm only human."

Where did that first microorganism, parent of us all, come from? Nobody knows, and in the circumstance it's anyone's guess, and the guesses abound. Francis Crick suggests that the improbability of its forming itself here on earth is so high that we must suppose it drifted in from outer space, shifting the problem to scientists in some other part of the galaxy or beyond. Others assert that it happened here indeed, piecing itself together molecule by molecule, over a billion years of chance events under the influence of sunlight and lightning, finally achieving by pure luck the exactly right sequence of nucleotides, inside the exactly right sort of membrane, and we were on our way.

No doubt the first success occurred in water. And not much doubt that the first event, however it happened, was the only such event, the only success. It was the biological equivalent of the Big Bang of the cosmophysicists, very likely a singular phenomenon, a piece of unprecedented good luck never to be repeated. If the sheer improbability of the thing taking place more than once, spontaneously and by chance, were not enough, consider the plain fact that all the cells that came later, right up to our modern brain cells, carry the same strings of DNA and work by essentially the same genetic code. It is the plainest evidence of direct inheritance from a single parent. We are all in the same family—grasses, seagulls, fish, fleas and voting citizens of the republic.

I ought to be able to remember the family tie, since all my cells are alive with reminders. In almost everything they do to carry me along from one day to the next, they use the biochemical devices of their microbial forebears. Jesse Roth and his colleagues at the National Institutes of Health have shown that the kingdom of bacteria had already learned, long before nucleated cells like ours came on the scene, how to signal to each other by chemical messages, inventing for this purpose molecules like insulin and a brilliant array of the same peptides that I make use of today for instructing my brain cells in proper behavior.

More than this, I could not be here, blinking in the light, without the help of an immense population of specialized bacteria that swam into cells like mine around a billion years ago and stayed there, as indispensable lodgers, ever since, replicating on their own, generation after generation. These are my mitochondria, the direct descendants of the first bacteria that learned how to make use of oxygen for energy. They occupy all my cells, swarming from one part to another wherever there is work to do. I could not lift a finger without them, nor think a thought, nor can they live without me. We are symbionts, my mitochondria and I, bound together for the advance of the biosphere, living together in harmony, maybe even affection. For sure, I am fond of my microbial engines, and I assume they are pleased by the work they do for me.

Or is it necessarily that way, or the other way round? It could be, I suppose, that all of me is a sort of ornamented carapace for colonies of bacteria that decided, long ago, to make a try at real evolutionary novelty. Either way, the accommodation will do.

The plants are in the same situation. They have the same swarms of mitochondria in all their cells, and other foreign populations as well. Their chloroplasts, which do the work of tapping solar energy to make all sugar, are the offspring of ancient pigmented microorganisms called cyanobacteria, once known as blue-green algae. These were the first creatures to learn—at least 2.5 billion years ago—how to use carbon dioxide from the air and plain water, and sunlight, to manufacture food for the market.

I am obsessed by bacteria, not just my own and those of the horse chestnut tree in my backyard, but bacteria in general. We would not have nitrogen for the proteins of the biosphere without the nitrogen-fixing bacteria, most of them living like special tissues in the roots of legumes. We would never have decay; dead trees would simply lie there forever, and so would we, and nothing on earth would be recycled. We couldn't keep cows, for cattle can't absorb their kind of food until their intestinal bacteria have worked it over, and for the same reason there would be no termites to cycle the wood; they are, literally, alive with bacteria. We would not have luminous fish for our aquariums, for the source of that spectacular light around their eyes is their private colonies of luminescent bacteria. And we would never have obtained oxygen to breathe, for all the oxygen in our air is exhaled for our use by the photosynthetic microbes in the upper waters of the seas and lakes and in the leaves of forests.

It was not that we invented a sophisticated new kind of cell with a modern nucleus and then invited in the more primitive and simpler forms of life as migrant workers. More likely, the whole assemblage came together by the joining up of different kinds of bacteria; the larger cell, the original "host," may have been one that had lost its rigid wall and swelled because of this defect. Lynn Margulis has proposed that the spirochetes were part of the original committee, becoming the progenitors of the cilia on modern cells, also the organizers of meiosis and mitosis, the lining up of chromosomes, the allocation of DNA to progeny—in effect, the reading of all wills. If she is right about this, the spirochetes were the inventors of biological sex and all that, including conclusive death.

The modern cell is not the single entity we thought it was a few years ago. It is an organism in its own right, a condominium, run by trustees.

If all this is true, as I believe it to be, the life of the earth is more intimately connected than I used to think. This is another thing on my mind, so much in my head these days that it crowds out other thoughts I used to have, making me sit up straight now, bringing me to my feet and then knocking me off them. The world works. The whole earth is alive, all of a piece, one living thing, a creature.

It breathes for us and for itself, and what's more it regulates the breathing with exquisite precision. The oxygen in the air is not placed there at random, any old way; it is maintained at precisely the optimal concentration for the place to be livable. A few percentage points more than the present level and the forests would burst into flames; a few less and most life would strangle. It is held there, constant, by feedback loops of information from the conjoined life of the planet. Carbon dioxide, inhaled by the plants, is held at precisely the low level that would be wildly improbable on any lifeless planet. And this happens to be the right concentration for keeping the earth's temperature, including the heat of the oceans, exactly right. Methane, almost all of it the product of bacterial metabolism, contributes also to the greenhouse effect, and methane is held steady. Statesmen must keep a close eye on the numbers these days—we are already pushing up the level of CO_2 by burning too much fuel and cutting too much forest, and the earth may be in for a climatic catastrophe within the next century.

But there it is: except for our meddling, the earth is the most stable organism we can know about—a complex system, a vast intelligence, turning in the warmth of the sun, running its internal affairs with the near-infallibility of a huge computer. Not entirely infallible, however, on the paleontological record. Natural catastrophes occur, crashes, breakdowns in the system: ice ages, meteor collisions, volcanic eruptions, global clouding, extinctions of great masses of its living tissue. It goes *down*, as we say of computers, but never out, always up again with something new to display to itself.

The newest of all things, the latest novelty among its working parts, seems to be us—language-speaking, song-singing, tool-making, fire-warming, comfortable, warfaring mankind, and I am of that ilk.

I can't remember anything about learning language as a child. I do have a few memories of studying to read and write, age four or five, I think, but I have no earlier recollection at all of learning speech. This surprises me.

You'd think that the first word, the first triumphant finished sentence, would have been such a stunning landmark to remain fixed in memory forever, the biggest moment in life. But I have forgotten. Or perhaps it never embedded itself in my mind. Being human, I may have known all along about language, from the time of my first glimpse of human faces, and speech just came, as natural a thing to do as breathing. The reason I can't remember the learning process, the early mistakes, may be that at that time they were not mistakes at all, just the normal speech of childhood, no more memorable than the first drawn breath.

All my adult life I have hoped to speak French one day like a Frenchman, but I am near to giving up, troubled. Why should any small French child, knee high, be able to do so quickly something that I will never learn to do? Or, for that matter, any English or Turkish child living for a few months in Paris? I know the answer, but I don't much like to hear it, implying as it does that there are other knacks that I have lost as well. Childhood is the time for language, no doubt about it. Young children, the younger the better, are good at it, it is child's play; it is a one-time gift to the species, withdrawn sometime in adolescence, switched off, never to be regained. I must have had it once and spent it all on ordinary English.

I possessed a splendid collection of neurones, nested

in a center somewhere in my left hemisphere, probably similar to the center in a songbird's brain—also on his left side—used for learning the species' song while he was still a nestling. Like mine, the bird's center is only there for studying in childhood; if he hears the proper song at that stage he will have it in mind for life, ornamenting it later with brief arpeggios so that it becomes his own particular, self-specific song, slightly but perceptibly different from the song of all his relatives. But if he can't hear it as a young child, the center can't compose it on its own, and what comes out later when he is ready for singing and mating is an unmelodious buzzing noise. This is one of the saddest tales in experimental biology.

Children may do more than simply pick up the language, easily as breathing. Perhaps they make it in the first place, and then change it around as time goes by, so that today's speech will, as always, be needing scholars as translators centuries hence. Derek Bickerton, professor of linguistics at the University of Hawaii, has studied the emergence of a brand-new language called Hawaiian Creole, which spread across the islands sometime after 1880, when the plantations were opened up for sugar export and large numbers of polyglot workers came from abroad to work the fields. The languages brought in were Japanese, Chinese, Portuguese, Spanish and Korean, all added to the native

Hawaiian and the then-dominant English speech. For a while nobody could understand anyone else. Then, as always happens in such language crises, a form of pidgin English developed (pidgin is the mispronunciation of "business" English), not really a language, more a crude system for naming objects and pointing at work to be done, lacking structure and syntactical rules.

Within the next generation, between 1880 and the turn of the century, Hawaiian Creole appeared. This was a proper language, flexible and fluent, capable of saying anything that popped into the head, filled with subtle metaphors and governed by its own tight grammatical rules for sentence structure. It was a new language, borrowing its vocabulary from the original words in the various tongues but arranging them in novel strings and sentences. According to Bickerton, the new grammar resembles that of creoles in other places—the Seychelles, for instance, and places in New Guinea—formed by other multilanguage communities. It also resembles, he asserts, the kind of sentence structure used by all children as they grow up in the acquisition of their native speech.

Hawaiian Creole was entirely new to the islands, in the important sense that it could not be understood or spoken by the adults of the community. Bickerton's conclusion, logically enough, is that it had to be a language invented *de novo* by the young children of Hawaii. He uses this observation for the deduction that children must possess in their brains what he calls a "bioprogram" for language, a neural mechanism for generating grammar (and a confirmation, on the facts, of Noam Chomsky's insight three decades ago).

If Bickerton is right, the way is open for a new kind of speculation about one of humanity's deepest secrets: How did language first develop? Who started all the talking, and under what circumstances? The story, I believe, tells itself.

I imagine a time, thousands of years ago, when there were only a million or so humans on the earth, mostly scattered and out of touch, traveling in families from place to place in search of food—hunters and gatherers. Nobody spoke, but there were human sounds everywhere: grunts, outcries imitating animals and birds, expletives with explanatory gestures. Very likely, our ancestors were an impatient, frantic lot, always indignant with each other for lacking understanding. Only recently down from the trees, admiring their apposing thumbs, astonished by intelligence, already studying fire, they must have been wondering what was missing and what was coming next. Probably they had learned to make the sounds needed for naming things—trees, plants, animals, fish—but no real speech, nothing like language.

Then they began settling down in places for longer

stays, having invented the beginnings of agriculture. More families gathered together, settled in communities. More children were born, and ways had to be found to keep the youngest ones safe from predators and out of the way of the adults. Corrals were constructed, fenced in, filled with children at play.

I imagine one special early evening, the elders sitting around the fire, grunting monosyllables, pointing at the direction of the next day's hunt or the next field to be slashed, thinking as hard as human beings can think when they are at a permanent loss for words. Then more noise than usual from the children's quarters, interrupting the thought. A rising surf of voices, excited, high-pitched, then louder and louder, exultant, totally incomprehensible to all the adults. Language.

It must have been resisted at first, regarded as nonsense. Perhaps resented, even feared, seeing it work so beautifully for communication but only among the children. Magic. Then, later on, accepted as useful magic, parts of it learned by some of the adults from their own children, broken creole. Words became magical, sentences were miraculous, grammar was sacred. (The thought hangs on: the Scottish cognate for grammar is "glamour," with the under-meaning of magic with words.)

"Kwei," said a Proto-Indo-European child, meaning

"make something," and the word became, centuries later, our word "poem."

But how did the children get it? I imagine they had it all the time, and have it still, latent in their brains, ready to make the words and join them together—to articulate, as we say. What was needed at the outset was a sufficient concentration of young children, a critical mass, at each other day after day, experimenting, trying words out for sense.

Whatever happened in the human brain to make this talent a possibility remains a mystery. It might have been a mutation, a new set of instructions in our DNA for the construction of a new kind of center, absent in all earlier primates. Or it could have been a more general list of specifications: i.e., don't stop now, keep making more columnar modules of neurons, build a bigger brain. Perhaps any brain with a rich enough cortex can become a speaking brain, with a self-conscious mind.

It is a satisfying notion for a memoir. I come from ancestors whose brains evolved so far beyond those of all their relatives that speech was the result, and with this in hand they became the masters of the earth, God's image, self-aware, able to remember generations back and to think generations ahead, able to write things like "In the beginning was the word." Nothing lies any longer beyond reach, not even the local solar system or out into the galaxy and even, given time, beyond that for colonizing the Universe. In charge of everything.

But this kind of talk is embarrassing; it is the way children talk before they've looked around. I must mend the ways of my mind. This is a very big place, and I don't know how it works, nor how I fit in. I am a member of a fragile species, still new to the earth, the youngest creatures of any scale, here only a few moments as evolutionary time is measured, a juvenile species, a child of a species. We are only tentatively set in place, error-prone, at risk of fumbling, in real danger at the moment of leaving behind only a thin layer of our fossils, radioactive at that.

With so much more to learn, looking around, we should be more embarrassed than we are. We are different, to be sure, but not so much because of our brains as because of our discomfiture, mostly with each other. All the other parts of the earth's life seem to get along, to fit in with each other, to accommodate, even to concede when the stakes are high. They live off each other, devour each other, scramble for ecological niches, but always within set limits, with something like restraint. It is a rough world, by some of our standards, but not the winner-take-all game that it seemed to us a while back. If we look over our shoulders as far as we can see, all the way past trillions of other species to those fossil stromatolites built by enormous communities of collaborating microorganisms, we can see no evidences of meanness or vandalism in nature. It is, on balance, an equable, generally amiable place—good-natured, as we say.

We are the anomalies for the moment, the self-conscious children at the edge of the crowd, unsure of our place, unwilling to join up, tending to grabbiness. We have much more to learn than language.

But we are not as bad a lot as some of us say. I don't agree with this century's fashion of running down the human species as a failed try, a doomed sport. At our worst, we may be going through the early stages of a species' adolescence, and everyone remembers what that is like. Growing up is hard times for an individual but sustained torment for a whole species, especially one as brainy and nervous as ours. If we can last it out, get through the phase, shake off the memory of this century, wait for a break, we may find ourselves off and running again.

This is an optimistic, Panglossian view, and I'm quick to say that I could be all wrong. Perhaps we have indeed come our full evolutionary distance, stuck forever with our present behavior, as mature as we ever will be for as long as we last. I doubt it. We are not out of options.

I am just enough persuaded by the sociobiologists to believe that our attitudes toward each other are influenced by genes, and by more than just the genes for making grammar. If these alone were our only wired-in guides to behavior, we would be limited to metaphor and ambiguity for our most important messages to each other. I think we do some other things, by nature.

From earliest infancy on, we can smile and laugh without taking lessons, we recognize faces and facial expressions, and we hanker for friends and company. It goes too far to say that we have genes for liking each other, but we tend in that direction because of being a biologically social species. I am sure of that point: we are more compulsively social, more interdependent and more inextricably attached to each other than any of the celebrated social insects. We are not, I fear, even marginally so committed to altruism as a way of life as the bees or ants, but at least we are able to sense, instinctively, certain obligations to one another.

One human trait, urging us on by our nature, is the drive to be useful, perhaps the most fundamental of all our biological necessities. We make mistakes with it, get it wrong, confuse it with self-regard, even try to fake it, but it is there in our genes, needing only a better set of definitions for usefulness than we have yet agreed on.

So we are not entirely set in our ways. Some of us may have more dominant genes for getting along than others. I suspect, glancing around my life, that we are also endowed with other, inhibitory alleles, widely spread for the enhancement of anomie. Most of us are a mixture. If we like, we can sit tight, trusting nature for the best of possible worlds to come. Or we can hope for better breeding, in both senses of the term, as our evolution proceeds.

Our microbial ancestors made use of quicker ways for bypassing long stretches of evolutionary time, and I envy them. They have always had an abundance of viruses, darting from one cell to another across species lines, doing no damage most of the time ("temperate" viruses, as they are called), but always picking up odds and ends of DNA from their hosts and then passing these around, as though at a great party. The bits are then used by the recipients for their betterment—new tricks for coping with new contingencies.

I hope our species has a mechanism like this. Come to think of it, maybe we do. After all, we live in a sea of our own viruses, most of which seem to be there for no purpose, not even to make us sick. We can hope that some of them might be taking hold of useful items of genetic news from time to time, then passing these along for the future of the species.

It makes a cheerful footnote, anyway: next time you feel a cold coming on, reflect on the possibility that you may be giving a small boost to evolution.

Bibliography

When we were planning this series of talks, it occurred to us that we would like to know what books our authors consulted or remembered or somehow found helpful in writing their own memoirs. We asked them for an informal list of their favorite first-person narratives or other works that influenced their writing. This bibliography is their answer to our request.

RUSSELL BAKER

Here are some of the books that were valuable to me during the writing of *Growing Up:*

Not So Wild a Dream by Eric Sevareid (Atheneum, 1976), *Personal History* by Vincent Sheean (Doubleday, Doran & Co., 1936), and *In Search of History* by Theodore H. White (Harper & Row, 1978). All three are journalists' memoirs

distinguished by a great deal of frankness about their child-
hoods and private lives. After thirty-three years as a newspaperman I had trouble writing candidly about my "personal
history" and found encouragement to try it anyhow in these
fine books by three of our best journalists.

Exiles (Farrar, Straus & Giroux, 1970) and *Passage to
Ararat* (Farrar, Straus & Giroux, 1975), both by Michael J.
Arlen. The prose is so good that I couldn't help writing a
little better after reading them. The books are models of how
to write about sensitive family relationships and the most
private emotions without falling into squalor and vulgarity.

The Dream of Golden Mountains by Malcolm Cowley (Viking Press, 1980) and *Starting Out in the Thirties* by Alfred
Kazin (Little, Brown, 1965). Because I wanted to create a
sense of what the Great Depression meant to adults and had
only a child's memory of it, I looked for memoirs by people
who had been adults in the 1930s. These were two of the
best. Because they dealt with an urban, intellectual America
totally different from anything I'd been aware of in the
1930s, they helped me understand the simplicity of the
world of my childhood.

Because so much of the book would be about my parents'
generation, which came to maturity during World War I
and the Jazz Age, I looked for material that would convey
a sense of how that period might have shaped people. The
best of it included:

Exile's Return by Malcolm Cowley (Viking Press, 1934;
revised, 1951) and *The Twenties* by Edmund Wilson (Farrar,

Straus & Giroux, 1975), with their picture of New York's literary Bohemia. It was startling to be reminded that the twentieth century was already blazing away so furiously just 250 miles north of the rustic backwater where my family was still living so close to the nineteenth.

The Mauve Decade by Thomas Beer (Alfred A. Knopf, 1926) was valuable in helping me understand the social tyranny exercised by women during the 1890s, when my mother was born, and how that tradition might have been passed on to her.

Goodbye to All That by Robert Graves (Jonathan Cape, 1929), *The Great War and Modern Memory* by Paul Fussell (Oxford University Press, 1975), and *Memoirs of an Infantry Officer* (Faber & Faber, 1930) and *Sherston's Progress* (Faber & Faber, 1936), both by Siegfried Sassoon, are invaluable to an understanding of how World War I shattered the nineteenth-century sensibility and prepared us for twentieth-century brutality.

The Rise of Theodore Roosevelt by Edmund Morris (Coward, McCann & Geoghegan, 1979) conveys a marvelous sense of the optimism that characterized the American spirit before World War I and makes it easier to understand how devastating the Great Depression must have been to adults born at the start of the century.

Not having written much in a personal vein until I started the book, I read many books to see how the thing was done, to see if I could discover the trick, as it were. The best of these were:

Dispatches by Michael Herr (Alfred A. Knopf, 1977), a report from Vietnam by a man trapped inside a nightmare. This extraordinarily personal piece of war reporting triumphs because the writer is scrupulously honest about his own terror, fatigue, ignorance, cowardice and anger.

Happy Days, 1880–1892 (Alfred A. Knopf, 1940) and *Newspaper Days, 1899–1906* (Alfred A. Knopf, 1941) by H. L. Mencken. Mencken does it like nobody else. As I discovered after several false starts, though, if you try to do it Mencken's way, you will produce only a very inferior counterfeit.

The Years with Ross by James Thurber (Little, Brown, 1959). Thurber wrote better than almost anybody, and I believe writers should always read their betters. It reminds them that they're not quite as good as they think they are.

Roughing It (F. G. Gilman & Co., 1872) and *Life on the Mississippi* (J. S. Osgood & Co., 1883) by Mark Twain. Nobody understood better than Twain that a memoir is not biography, but an art form. What a pleasure to watch him improve dull stretches of arid fact with inventions of the mind. I also discovered that even the greatest writer can be defeated by insensate demands of editors. The last half of *Life on the Mississippi* is heavy going because an editor wanted it to be twice as long as it should have been.

Autobiography by Anthony Trollope (Williams & Norgate Ltd., 1887). Looking for tips from the most relentless writer ever, I found only advice to write relentlessly. It is, however, a fascinating look at a literary life built on the work ethic, and a valuable book for all writers to know about. When asked, "How can I become a writer?" I now reply, "Read Trollope's autobiography; the secret is there."

Autobiography (various versions have appeared under different titles from c. 1791) by Benjamin Franklin. I intended to write about this in the book and wanted to know if it was as hard to stay awake through as it was in my childhood. The answer was: not quite.

Remembrance of Things Past (Bernard Grasset, vol. I; La Nouvelle Revue Française, vols. II–VII, 1914–1927; Holt & Co., 1922; Random House, 1932) by Marcel Proust. This is the ultimate memoir. Proust's ability to startle the reader with some revelatory scene that suddenly casts everything in a new light is a gift I envy. I read through all seven very long volumes again in search of the secret. I had a wonderful time, while learning that I might just possibly achieve Proust's effects if I wrote seven very long volumes, though it was unlikely. So I wrote only one rather short volume.

ANNIE DILLARD

These are some first-person narratives I dearly love:

NINETEENTH-CENTURY UNITED STATES

The Education of Henry Adams (Houghton Mifflin, 1918). I like its vigorous thought and its assumption that an account of one's intellectual life is indeed an account of one's life.

Henry David Thoreau, *Walden* (Ticknor & Fields, 1854).

In its formal shapeliness and metaphorical, hyperbolic prose it far exceeds the scrapbook journals as the monument of Thoreau the artist.

Richard Henry Dana, *Two Years Before the Mast* (Harper & Brothers, 1840).

Mark Twain, *Life on the Mississippi* (J. S. Osgood & Co., 1883).

TWENTIETH-CENTURY UNITED STATES

Alfred Kazin, *A Walker in the City* (Harcourt, Brace, 1951). This stirringly illustrates a paradox on which, I think, the finest autobiographical literature depends, that is, that the life of the spirit, which in an adult often becomes the life of the mind, enters the child through the senses. I have read this book over and over again.

Russell Baker, *Growing Up* (Congdon & Weed, 1982). Most of the best memoirs, like this vivid and genial one, refrain from examining the self at all.

James McConkey, *Court of Memory* (Dutton, 1983). A recent and elegiac account of a calm life lived deeply. I admire its structural integrity and literary intelligence. More and more I find these aesthetic satisfactions in nonfiction; essayists and other nonfiction writers are taking the care and perhaps practicing the artifices that English prose writers used to practice in the seventeenth century. Many fiction writers whose work sees print apparently are not.

Mary Heaton Vorse, *Time and the Town: A Provincetown Chronicle* (Dial Press, 1942). Like Marjorie Kinnan Rawlings's *Cross Creek* (Charles Scribner's Sons, 1942) in its broad-spirited re-creation of energetic and hospitable decades among friends.

The Autobiography of Malcolm X (Grove Press, 1965). A magnificent narrative.

Norman MacLean, *A River Runs Through It* (University of Chicago Press, 1976). Published as fiction, this reads like the best of memoirs. It is a favorite of many writers.

Lewis Thomas, *The Youngest Science* (Oxford University Press, 1983). The genial medical researcher remembers the medicine of his father's day and the researches of his own. A matter-of-fact quality to his writing and a pure, clean attention to the materials at hand make Lewis Thomas's writing modest, honest and serious.

Frank Conroy, *Stop-Time* (Viking Press, 1967). Conroy masters a narrative, dramatic, novelistic handling of scenes.

Booker T. Washington, *Up from Slavery* (Doubleday, Page & Co., 1901). This classic holds up; it is a pleasure to read.

Henry Beston, *The Outermost House* (Doubleday, Doran & Co., 1928). This Cape Cod masterpiece is broad and simple. Its power derives from two images: the cold, pagan stars and the fateful, killing waves.

Maureen Howard, *Facts of Life* (Little, Brown, 1978). Howard grew up in Bridgeport, Connecticut, among a variety of colorful people she describes with insight.

Maxine Hong Kingston, *The Woman Warrior* (Alfred A. Knopf, 1976). There is a long story in here about a Chinese aunt that is one of the funniest stories I've seen in print. Kingston is a sophisticated and original writer.

Thomas Merton, *The Seven Storey Mountain* (Harcourt, Brace, 1948). Merton's account of the steps that led him from a privileged childhood in France, through Columbia University and to a Trappist monastery in Kentucky.

James Thurber, *My Life and Hard Times* (Harper & Brothers, 1933). This is vintage Thurber.

Ethel Waters, *His Eye Is on the Sparrow* (Doubleday, 1951). The singer Ethel Waters tells her moving story of music, hardship and faith.

Kate Simon, *Bronx Primitive* (Viking Press, 1982). A vivid, rough-and-tumble childhood in a Bronx immigrant neighborhood in the 1930s.

AND ABROAD

John Cowper Powys, *Autobiography* (John Lane, 1934). An extreme of the genre, written with the usual Powys restrictions. In this case he belabors his so-called eroticism and omits all mention of the women in his life. The oddest of this great writer's many odd books.

Edwin Muir, *An Autobiography* (Hogarth Press, 1954). A beautiful evocation of the timelessness of early childhood, in the Orkney Islands, by the poet and translator of Kafka.

Ved Mehta, *Vedi* (Oxford University Press, 1982). In beautiful, formal, vivid language, the writer describes his blind, vigorous boyhood in India.

Kildare Dobbs, *Running to Paradise* (Oxford University

Press, 1962). The Canadian man of letters recounts his travels and impressions following his immigration from Northern Ireland.

Nikos Kazantzakis, *Report to Greco* (Simon & Schuster, 1965). This strong, storyteller's autobiography escapes the usual hazards of Kazantzakis.

Maxim Gorky, the trilogy: *My Childhood* (T. W. Laurie, 1915); *My Apprenticeship* (Foreign Languages Publishing House, 1952, also as *In the World*, The Century Co., 1917); *My Universities* (Boni & Liveright, 1923). Gorky's childhood was actually colorful; his father was a dyer, and the dye vats in the yard stained everything. The usual Russian extremes of living and of writing are right here.

Graham Greene, *A Sort of Life* (Bodley Head, 1971). An austere, intelligent autobiography.

Pablo Neruda, *Memoirs* (Farrar, Straus & Giroux, 1977). The poet writes a muscular prose; he describes the literary camaraderie of his early manhood in Valparaíso.

C. S. Lewis, *Surprised by Joy* (Harcourt Brace Jovanovich, 1955). The Christian's intellectual autobiography begins with a happy boyhood.

Wilfrid Sheed, *Frank and Maisie* (Simon & Schuster, 1985). His parents were low-church British evangelists, great and lively characters.

Vladimir Nabokov, *Speak, Memory* (Putnam, 1966). Nabokov's memoir of old Russia is pure description, emotional in its spareness. He describes a needlepoint chair seat.

Jean-Paul Sartre, *The Words* (Gallimard, 1964; George

Braziller, 1964). Sartre's original memoir is, I think, his best, most literary work.

Antoine de Saint-Exupéry, *Wind, Sand and Stars* (Gallimard, 1939; Reynal & Hitchcock, 1939). In the early days of aviation the author flew the mails over North Africa. A dandy book.

ALFRED KAZIN

Because of the Puritan passion for constantly keeping in mind the report of one's doings and misdemeanors to be delivered to Almighty God, American writing is especially rich in journals and memoirs from the earliest period. The journals of Ralph Waldo Emerson (Houghton Mifflin, 1909–1914); Henry David Thoreau, one of the longest ever kept (Houghton Mifflin, 1906); Walt Whitman's *Specimen Days* (Donald McKay, 1882); John Quincy Adams's diaries, sometimes called "Memoirs" and supposed to be the longest journal ever kept by a public man (J. B. Lippincott & Co., 1874–1877), are all conscious autobiographies in this sense.

I have been preoccupied much of my life with this literature, probably because I have kept a journal since I was in knee pants, and because my interest in American literature keeps returning to the "personal"—by which I mean "the self as history."

American classics in this context: *The Education of Henry Adams* (Houghton Mifflin, 1918)—to me the most wonderful example of how to see one's life as history.

Earlier, of course, *The Autobiography of Benjamin Franklin,* the prototypical story of the self-made American, but distinctive also for its wry humor.

Theodore Dreiser's *Dawn* (Horace Liveright, 1931). There is nothing else like it for portraying the "provincial" seizing for wonder and literary inspiration upon the "Big City" (Chicago).

Hemingway's *A Moveable Feast* (Charles Scribner's Sons, 1964). Full of lies or shall we say delusions, but marvelous nonetheless because it shows the same artifice of genius that went to make up his classic short stories.

Moving about at random, I would also include Malcolm X's *Autobiography* (Grove Press, 1965). I am aware that he had a lot of "help" in this, to put it gently, but it is the best story I know of the black experience in America from a purely personal, sensory point of view. Though of course I have to add Richard Wright's *Black Boy* (Harper & Brothers, 1945). Wright remains in my mind the most gifted of all twentieth-century black American writers.

I have forgotten such central items in American autobiography as *The Autobiography of Lincoln Steffens* (Harcourt, Brace, 1931), a classic portrait of American politics, urban scandals and Steffens's own utopian self-delusions on the subject of Soviet Russia, which are now as funny as they are sad.

One can hardly omit from any table of American autobiography such succulent dishes as Whitman's *Leaves of Grass* (Fowler & Wells, 1855), Thoreau's *Walden* (Ticknor & Fields, 1854), Saul Bellow's *The Adventures of Augie*

March (Viking Press, 1953) and *Herzog* (Viking Press, 1964), and Robert Lowell's *Life Studies* (Farrar, Straus & Cudahy, 1959). There is no need, perhaps, to go on in this vein—Sylvia Plath, James Merrill, Anne Sexton, etc., etc.

The prime example in modern European literature of the novel as autobiography, the autobiography as novel, is Proust's *Remembrance of Things Past.* Proust's great biographer, George Painter, said he documented much of his biography from the novel!

TONI MORRISON

As Toni Morrison points out in her talk, a large part of her literary heritage consists of the book-length narratives that were written by slaves in the eighteenth and nineteenth centuries. Well over a hundred were published, she says, and she names the ones that have been particularly important to her as a writer. She also mentions several influential books by modern writers such as Simone de Beauvoir and James Baldwin. Her talk is her bibliography.

LEWIS THOMAS

For the bibliography, I suggest the following:

Most of my reading time is spent on journals: *Nature, Science, Cell, Cellular Immunology, Journal of Experimental*

Medicine, PNAS (Proceedings of the National Academy of Science), several others for library browsing.

The books I keep near at hand, late nights and weekends:

American Heritage Dictionary (the earliest editions containing Calvert Watkins's section on philology and Indo-European roots).

The Roots of Language, by Derek Bickerton (Karoma Publishers, Ann Arbor, 1981). Here is the evidence for the role of children in Creole language formation.

Insect Societies, by E. O. Wilson. Models for complex social systems, beautifully illustrated.

Symbiosis in Cell Evolution, by Lynn Margulis, and *Microcosmos,* by Margulis and Dorion Sagan. The mechanism of interliving is the most important problem for modern biology, just beginning to open up.

Wallace Stevens, all editions.

Part of Nature, Part of Us, by Helen Vendler, the most interesting critic alive.

Montaigne, the Donald Frame translation.

The Spectator Bird (and other assorted novels) by Wallace Stegner.

E. M. Forster, all of, for picking up anywhere.

WILLIAM ZINSSER

Two of my favorite memoirs are by writers who gave talks in this series: Russell Baker's *Growing Up* and Alfred Kazin's *A Walker in the City.* Here are a dozen others that

I enjoyed with unusual intensity when I first encountered them and that I still remember vividly as models of the form.

Arlen, Michael J. *Exiles* (Farrar, Straus & Giroux, 1970). A stylish and sensitive recollection of a father and mother who were known on two continents for their glamour and of what it was like to be their son.

Behrman, S. N. *People in a Diary: A Memoir* (Little, Brown, 1972). An extraordinary gallery of famous friends—most memorably, the young Siegfried Sassoon and the dying George Gershwin—recalled with charm and warmth by Behrman from the diary he kept for fifty years.

Doctorow, E. L. *World's Fair* (Random House, 1985). Posing as a novel, this minutely observed reconstruction of a Bronx boyhood in the thirties, culminating in the great New York World's Fair of 1939, has too much truth not to be true.

Hart, Moss. *Act One* (Random House, 1959). One of America's most successful playwrights had a New York boyhood of such grinding poverty that the memory of it, as told here with a born dramatist's sense of timing and surprise, still haunts and troubles me.

Houseman, John. *Run-Through: A Memoir* (Simon & Schuster, 1972). The author's role as midwife to such innovative productions as the Virgil Thomson–Gertrude Stein opera *Four Saints in Three Acts,* the WPA's Negro Theatre Project and Orson Welles's Mercury Theatre and *Citizen Kane* is recalled with gusto and a remembered enjoyment of huge risks gladly taken.

Lee, Laurie. *The Edge of Day—A Boyhood in the West of England* (William Morrow, 1960). Thinly disguised as prose, this evocation of growing up in the Cotswolds has the richness and imagery of poetry. I still remember being affected by the seemingly effortless beauty of its language.

Mencken, H. L. *Happy Days, 1880–1892* (Alfred A. Knopf, 1940); *Newspaper Days, 1899–1906* (Knopf, 1941); and *Heathen Days, 1890–1936* (Knopf, 1943). These peppery memoirs, which I first found in Armed Forces Editions during World War II, brightened many long nights in North Africa and Italy with their exuberant style, reinforcing, among other things, my dream of becoming a newspaperman when the war was over. In 1980, twenty chapters from the three volumes were published in a book called *A Choice of Days* (Knopf), selected and introduced by Edward L. Galligan.

Mortimer, John. *Clinging to the Wreckage: A Part of a Life* (Ticknor & Fields, 1982). The son of a blind barrister who specialized in divorce cases whose lurid details had to be read aloud to him, Mortimer—a barrister himself and also a prolific author and playwright—has written a memoir that is both tender and hilarious.

Nabokov, Vladimir. *Speak, Memory* (Putnam, 1966). Although English was Nabokov's fourth language, no English or American author has written a more elegant memoir than this meticulous recollection of a golden childhood—a world of private tutors and summer houses—in czarist St. Petersburg.

Origo, Iris. *Images & Shadows: Part of a Life* (Harcourt Brace Jovanovich, 1971). The wise and graceful memoir of an American who grew up partly in Ireland and Europe, married an Italian, and created a life on a farm in Tuscany that had many fulfillments, not the least being the chance to hide Italian partisans and Allied soldiers during the Nazi occupation of World War II.

Pritchett, V. S. *A Cab at the Door* (Random House, 1968). Pritchett recalls a boyhood that was almost Dickensian in its hardship—his apprenticeship to the London leather trade belongs to the nineteenth century—without self-pity and even with a certain merriment and gratitude. A wonderful memoir.

Woolf, Leonard. *Growing: An Autobiography of the Years 1904–1911* (Harcourt, Brace & World, 1962). The second of an eventual six memoirs by the man Virginia Woolf would marry. This volume is my favorite because it compresses one man's exotic experience—Woolf's years as a young British civil servant in a village in Ceylon—and by extension tells the story of all the earnest colonials who have found themselves trying to administer justice in strange and bewildering lands.

Contributors

RUSSELL BAKER was born in rural Virginia in 1925, spent two years training as a Navy flier in World War II, graduated from Johns Hopkins University in 1947 and began his newspaper career with the Baltimore *Sun*. In 1954 he joined the *New York Times* and covered the White House, the Senate, the State Department and several presidential campaigns before starting in 1962 his thrice-weekly column, "Observer," for which he subsequently won the Pulitzer Prize. He has published eleven books, most recently *The Norton Book of Light Verse*, which he edited. He is now working on a second autobiographical memoir, this one about the glory of being a young newspaperman in the golden-age America of the 1950s. He lives with his wife, Miriam, in northern Virginia near the village where he was born.

ANNIE DILLARD's *Pilgrim at Tinker Creek* won the
Pulitzer Prize for nonfiction in 1974 and has since been
translated into many languages. Her other books include a
book of poetry, a book of literary theory and a book of essays
(*Teaching a Stone to Talk*) that originally appeared in leading
magazines and that have also been widely reprinted in anthologies. Her most recent book is *Encounters with Chinese
Writers.* She has been awarded fellowships from the National Endowment for the Arts and the John Simon Gug-
genheim Foundation. She is a winner of the New York
Press Club Award for Excellence and a Washington Gover-
nor's Award. In 1982 she delivered the Phi Beta Kappa
Oration at the commencement exercises of Harvard University. She lives in New England with her husband, Gary
Clevidence, and their daughter, Rosie.

ALFRED KAZIN was born in Brooklyn, graduated
from the City College of New York, and began his career
as literary editor of *The New Republic* in 1942. He was
Distinguished Professor of English at the State University
of New York in Stony Brook from 1963 to 1973 and at the
City University of New York Graduate Center from 1973
to 1985. He has also been a visiting professor at many universities here and abroad. Among his books are three memoirs—*A Walker in the City, Starting Out in the Thirties* and
New York Jew—and such major works of literary criticism
as *On Native Grounds* and *An American Procession.* He has

also edited anthologies and critical studies of such writers as Emerson, Melville, Hawthorne, Henry James and F. Scott Fitzgerald. He is a member of the American Academy and Institute of Arts and Letters.

TONI MORRISON was born in Lorain, Ohio, graduated from Howard University and received her master's degree from Cornell. As an editor at Random House for many years she brought to publication such writers as Toni Cade Bambara, Angela Davis and Gayl Jones. She has taught at many universities, including Yale, Rutgers and Stanford, and is now Schweitzer Professor in the College of Humanities and Fine Arts at the State University of New York in Albany. Her novels include *The Bluest Eye, Sula, Song of Solomon,* which won the National Book Critics Circle Award in 1978, and *Tar Baby.* Her new novel, *Beloved,* will be published this year. She is also the author of a play, *Dreaming Emmett.* She holds eleven honorary degrees and is a member of the American Academy and Institute of Arts and Letters and a trustee of the New York Public Library. She lives in Rockland County, N.Y.

LEWIS THOMAS, president emeritus of Memorial Sloan-Kettering Cancer Center, was born in Flushing, N.Y., graduated from Princeton University and got his M.D. degree from Harvard. He has been on the faculty of five schools of medicine and dean of two of them: N.Y.U.–Bellevue Medical Center and the Yale School of Medicine. He has published more than 200 scientific papers on virology, immunology, experimental pathology and infectious disease, has received more than twenty honorary degrees, and has served on many government advisory committees. He received the National Book Award for *Lives of a Cell* and the American Book Award for *The Medusa and the Snail*. His two most recent books are a memoir of his career, *The Youngest Science*, and a collection of essays, *Late Night Thoughts on Listening to Mahler's Ninth Symphony*.

WILLIAM ZINSSER, general editor of the Book-of-the-Month Club, spent the first thirteen years of his career with the New York *Herald Tribune* as a writer, editor and critic. He left the paper in 1959 to become a freelance writer and has since written regularly for leading magazines. From 1968 to 1972 he wrote a column for *Life*. During the 1970s he was at Yale University, where he taught nonfiction writing and humor writing and was master of Branford College. He is the author of eleven books, including the classic *On Writing Well* and *Willie and Dwike*, a portrait of the jazz musicians Willie Ruff and Dwike Mitchell. He also edited *Extraordinary Lives*, the book derived from the first series of talks sponsored by the Book-of-the-Month Club, on the art and craft of biography. He lives in New York, his home town, with his wife, Caroline Zinsser.